AN ISLANDER'S

Guide to Writing

Edited by

Susan Wolff Murphy

Texas A & M University, Corpus Christi

FOUNTAINHEAD
PRESS

Cover Image courtesy of Texas A & M University, Corpus Christi
Some Material Provided by Fountainhead Press

Cover design by Doris Bruey
Text design by Patricia Bracken

Books may be purchased for educational purposes.

For information, please call or write:

1-800-586-0330

Fountainhead Press
100 W. Southlake Blvd. Suite 142, #350
Southlake, TX 76092

Web site: www.fountainheadpress.com
Email: customerservice@fountainheadpress.com

ISBN 978-1-59871-274-2

Table of Contents

WELCOME TO THE FIRST-YEAR WRITING PROGRAM

at

Texas A&M University-Corpus Christi

Fall 2008

Dear First-Year Student-

If you have purchased this textbook, you are undoubtedly enrolled in First Year Composition (FYC) at Texas A&M University-Corpus Christi. Congrats, Islander! You're in for a great learning experience.

The focus of FYC is to help you develop and enhance your ability to use writing in a variety of situations, primarily academic. We assume that you have been writing in school for twelve years and know the basics. You've been a user of language for many years beyond that. Writing is central to our identities as human beings.

Writing is a tool we use to accomplish goals. We develop our ability to use writing over a lifetime; we are never finished learning to write, yet none of us are beginners.

The word, "writing," implies several behaviors; however, each writing task requires a writer to take stock, to assess, to decide which behaviors are appropriate and which are not. Any task is defined by many things: the purpose, the audience, the exigency, the discourse community, and the genre. These factors are all interdependent. Expert writers recognize all these factors on a more or less conscious level each time they write.

FYC focuses on the kinds of writing, reading, thinking and discussing that people do at the university. Most academic writing requires formal language, strict documentation, use and acknowledgement of sources, disciplinary conventions, and western conceptions of clarity and style.

FYC courses are going to ask you to ask questions, develop responses to issues, find evidence to support your responses, and incorporate those sources into complex written genres. The courses will require you to consider multiple perspectives, to respect difference, and to add shades of gray to almost any discussion of social issues.

These courses are committed to the idea that writing is an act of communication between people, that it is context and purpose specific, and that to be an effective writer you must understand in which discourse community you are writing. English 1301 and 1302 emphasize writing for different audiences, purposes, and contexts, using appropriate genres and conventions. You will deepen your understanding of and develop your use of writing processes that include invention, writing multiple drafts, sharing and responding to work in progress, revising, editing, and publishing. You will develop information literacy and engage in critical thinking as you work through writing and reading assignment sequences that require ongoing inquiry and problem solving.

The courses in the First Year Writing Program are:

English 1301

Research processes, the dynamics of rhetoric (audience and purpose, ethos/pathos/logos), and the 5 recursive "aspects" of the writing process (brainstorming, drafting, revising, editing, publishing): Wiki, WebCT, the Bedford Researcher, and Bell Library's databases.

English 1302

Rhetorical analysis, visual rhetoric, primary and secondary research, disciplinary differences in writing expectations, genre, and discourse community.

Most of our FYC courses are linked to other courses in learning communities. These links allow teachers to develop interdisciplinary assignments, discuss what writing expectations are in various contexts, and use writing to help you learn the subject areas you are studying.

I hope your FYC course is a learning experience in which you can refine your skills, find new ways to use writing, and expand the number of genres, purposes, and audiences with which you feel comfortable. My goal is to "set students on a course of life-long learning so that they know how to learn to become better and better writers in a variety of social contexts" and can therefore succeed as writers, students, and people (Beaufort, 2007, p. 7).

Sincerely,

Dr. Susan Wolff Murphy

FYWP Coordinator
Co-Director of the University Core Curriculum Program
Faculty Center 253A
(361) 825-2150

OUR RESPONSIBILITIES/YOUR RESPONSIBILITIES

As a reminder, this is college. You will encounter no "hand-holding" or "spoon-feeding." You will, however, encounter teachers who are more than willing to help you succeed when you have demonstrated that you are fulfilling your responsibility for your own success. Accordingly, the First Year Learning Communities Program expects you to become an independent learner, one who knows how to learn and how to take responsibility for your own success. We will not always answer your questions with the kinds of answers you expect. Instead, we may ask you further questions, or we may ask your classmates to help you arrive at answers. This is not because we don't care whether you pass or fail. We care very much about your success, and we want to help you become independent, responsible learners.

What We Expect from You

- To come to class every day thoroughly prepared. This means that you have read the assigned readings before class without me reminding you, you have posted or e-mailed all assigned out-of-class writings, and you are fully prepared to write and talk about the day's topics, readings and writings.
- To read all assignments carefully, and ask questions if you don't understand something—there are no dumb questions, no matter what you've heard to the contrary. Chances are, there are other people wondering the same thing. We only ask that your questions be specific, referring to the exact materials you don't understand and to what it is that you don't understand about the material. To help you, we will provide you with extensive explanations of written assignments and activities.
- To read the class plans every day, to closely follow the schedule of work that we have posted in each day's class plans, and to be aware of all assignments, activities, and changes to the daily plans that may have been made since the last time you looked at it. You will be held accountable for knowing about and submitting on time any work that's due. The class plans section will contain all the information you need to be active, engaged, and prepared for each day's class. Read it closely each day before coming to class! We cannot stress this enough.
- To conduct your research in a thoughtful and scholarly manner, which includes giving credit to your sources, following a reasonable schedule, being consistent with your work, not putting things off, and upholding all academic standards for professionalism and ethics.
- To treat your peers and me with respect, even if our world views, values, and opinions are wildly different from yours. Please be tolerant of others.
- To be a thoughtful reader of the work of your peers. Sharing writing is an intimate activity, and is a difficult thing for some people to do. So, you should be constructive and positive in your critiques. When we do peer review activities, always give the writer thoughtful, concrete suggestions, and always give the writer's piece as much time and attention as you would want your readers to give yours.
- To communicate with your teachers. If there is something that is going on in your life that is affecting your work, please let them know as soon as possible. If you repeatedly miss class or fail to turn in assignments without notifying your teachers of some difficulty you may be having, no matter how "small," so that they can help you, they will assume that you aren't interested in succeeding. And ALWAYS REMEMBER, if you don't understand or are having trouble completing an assignment FOR ANY REASON, please let your teachers know, so they can help.

What You Should Expect from Your Teachers:

- To come to class every day thoroughly prepared. This means that we will have thoughtfully and carefully prepared each day's lesson plans so that they not only meet the goals and objectives of the course, but also, and most importanly, meet your needs in a way that furthers your learning.
- To help you learn to conduct research in a thorough and scholarly manner.
- To treat you with respect, even if your world view, values, and opinions are wildly different from ours.
- To be a thoughtful reader and evaluator of your work. We know that some of the things you share with me are personal or sensitive, and we fully respect your decision to share them with me. Therefore, we will not share anything you write or tell me with anyone else without your direct permission. We will treat all of your writing with the respect and care that it deserves.
- To communicate honestly and openly with you. We will try our best to clearly communicate the assignments and requirements of the class in order for you to succeed to the best of your capabilities. If we think something outside of class is affecting our energy and enthusiasm on a particular day, we will tell you so. Your teachers like for you to know them as people, just as we like to know you. Therefore, we foster a classroom atmosphere of openness, honesty, and invitation. We want this to be a good experience for everyone!

Ashleigh Davis

CONTRIBUTORS

The First Year Writing Program faculty and students and Texas A&M University-Corpus Christi would like to thank our contributors very much for their additions to this textbook.

Thank you,

Glenn Blalock

Jen Bray

Ashleigh Davis

Tim Harlow

Frances Johnson

Vickie Machen

Orion Powell

CHAPTER 1

Overview

In the Beginning . . .

As a result of the *South Texas Border Initiative* meant to redress disparities in educational access, TAMU-CC developed the Core Curriculum and the First-Year Learning Communities Program, and in 1994, expanded to enroll first and second year students.

Learning communities have been described as "one of the most powerful interventions on the educational landscape because they provide a comprehensive, cost-effective framework for enhancing student learning" (Smith, MacGregor, Matthews, & Gabelnick (2004, p. 4).

The First-Year Learning Communities Program (FYLCP)

TAMU-CC's First-Year Learning Communitites Program (FYLCP) is an innovative program which helps students make successful academic and social transitions from high school to the University. In 2001, the Texas Higher Education Coordinating Board selected TAMU-CC's FYLCP to receive the Texas Higher Education Star Award. The Coordinating Board gave out only five Star Awards statewide, and the FYLCP was the only first-year program to win one. The program earned further recognition in 2002, this time at the national level: The Brevard College Policy Center on the First Year of College selected TAMU-CC from 130 nominees across the country, as one of the 13 "Institutions of Excellence in the First College Year."

What is a Learning Community?

In their first year, TAMU-CC students enroll in specially selected groups of 3 or 4 classes known as Triads and Tetrads. The students and teachers within each Triad or Tetrad form a *learning community*. The same group of students takes all of the classes within a given Triad or Tetrad together, which gives them many opportunities to work together, get to know each other, and learn together. The teachers in each learning community also work with each other, in order to develop connections among the classes: relating content, assignments, and activities in one class with content, assignments, and activities in other Triad or Tetrad classes.

Benefits of Learning Communities

TAMU-CC's learning communities program has been built upon years of research concerning learning communities. The research indicates that well-designed learning communities benefit students in many ways. For example, students who participate in learning communities:

- Have more opportunities to express themselves in writing and orally in academic contexts;

- Develop their academic skills more fully;
- Are more engaged or involved in learning experiences and in college life;
- Experience greater intellectual development;
- Report higher levels of satisfaction with their college or university;
- Are more likely to complete their courses and stay in school;
- And tend to earn higher grades.

Structure of the Triads and Tetrads

All of the Triads and Tetrads include a First-Year Seminar and a First-Year Composition class. These are small classes of 25 students or fewer. In addition, Triads include a large lecture class (such as General Psychology or U.S. Government and Politics), and Tetrads include two large lecture classes. The classes within each Triad (or Tetrad) are "linked," in the sense that students enroll in all three classes (or four classes in a Tetrad) at once, as a "package deal."

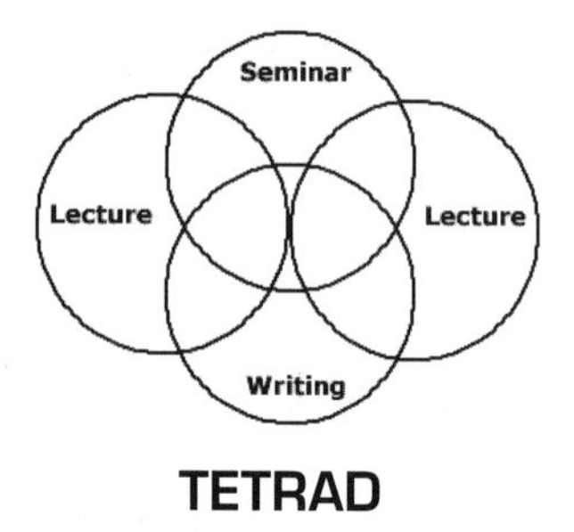

TETRAD

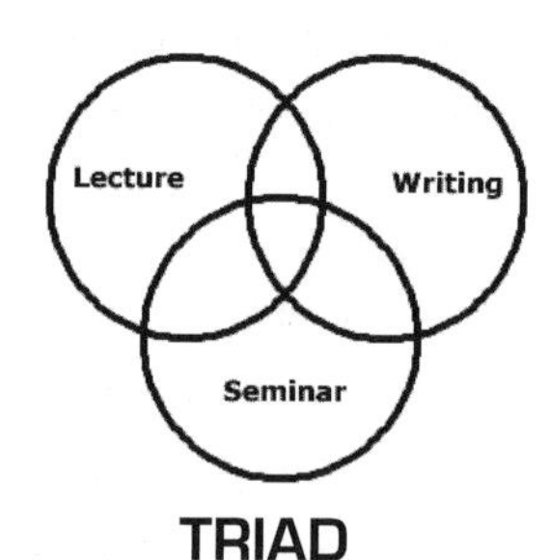

TRIAD

First-Year Seminar

First-Year Seminar (FYS) plays a central role in the development of the learning communities. FYS is designed to help students achieve success, academically and socially, as they make the transition from high school to the university. The primary objectives of FYS are for students to:

- Explore the interconnections among the Triad/Tetrad courses;
- Develop critical thinking skills and significant learning;
- Clarify personal values, goals, and strengths;
- And develop the ability to learn through study, discussion, writing, cooperation, and collaboration.

UCCP 1101. First-Year Seminar I

Interdisciplinary discussion of topics presented in the first-year Triad/Tetrad in which the student is concurrently enrolled. Required of full-time first-year students; to be taken as a component of the student's first Triad or Tetrad.

UCCP 1102. First-Year Seminar II

Continuation of UCCP 1101. Interdisciplinary discussion of topics presented in the first-year Triad/Tetrad in which the student is currently enrolled and use of bibliographic resources for research. Required of full-time first-year students; to be taken as a component of the student's second Triad or Tetrad.

The First Year Writing Program (FYWP)

FYWP courses introduce students to college-level writing, reading, researching, and thinking. Students explore different writing processes, use writing to learn, and learn to write for different audiences and purposes, including writing for courses across the curriculum and writing for audiences and purposes beyond the university. All first-year writing courses are taught in networked computer classrooms.

ENGL 1301. Composition I

Principles, techniques, and processes of written composition, textual analysis, and critical thinking. Satisfies the university core curriculum requirement in composition.

ENGL 1302. Composition II

Principles, techniques, and processes of written composition, with an emphasis on research and argument. Satisfies the university core curriculum requirement in composition. Prerequisite: ENGL 1301.

Online Courses

FYS and English 1301/1302 are offered every semester online. Permission is required. First-Year Seminar (UCCP 1101/1102) online is limited to upper-class students, non-traditional students, and those for whom a learning community is impossible. If you desire to take seminar online, please discuss it with your Academic Advisor to see if it is a good option for you. Once you are referred by your advisor, permits are given by Mr. Schwerin, the Program Coordinator, during registration for classes. If you have questions, please contact the FYLCP office at 825-2150.

English 1301 and English 1302 are offered online every fall and spring semester. Students in these courses have serious limitations on their time, might be part-time or non-traditional students, are retaking the course, or may opt for this option for another reason. If you desire to take composition online, please discuss it with your Academic Advisor to see if it is a good option. Once you are referred by your Advisor, permits are given by Mr. Schwerin, the Program Coordinator, during registration for classes. If you have questions, please contact the FYLCP office at 825-2150.

English 1301/1301 Learning Goals, Objectives and Outcomes

The list below represents the goals, objectives, and outcomes of each course in the program: English 1301 and English 1302 and offers ways that the FYWP articulates with the University's Core Curriculum.

Core Perspectives

- Explore differing perspectives on the relationship between self and society
- Understand the responsibilities of living and using language in a diversified world

- Discuss and reflect upon the individual, political, economic and social aspects of life to understand ways to be a responsible member of society
- Define and assess values for ethical behavior
- Understand the integral relationship of knowledge across the curriculum
- Develop an awareness of how technology affects our lives and the capacity to use it responsibly

FYWP Perspectives

- A significant strength of the First Year Writing Program lies in the diversity of the community it respects and serves
- Reading and writing as literate acts arise out of, shape and are shaped by contexts that are individual, social, political and historical
- Reading and writing are practices through which humans act and make meaning
- The writing classroom is a site of respectful and ethical interaction
- Writing, as primary medium for constructing knowledge, enhances learning across the curriculum
- Choices of writing and reading technology affect one's composing process

Core Learning Goals

- Understand and use writing and speaking processes of invention, drafting, revision, editing, and delivery
- Specify audience and purpose and make appropriate rhetorical choices
- Produce clear and coherent prose as adapted to purpose, audience and occasion
- Understand the importance of practice and reflection
- Read for a variety of purposes across the disciplines
- Understand research as inquiry and integral to one's writing processes
- Use critical reasoning for problem solving
- Evaluate arguments analytically and creatively
- Listen carefully, think critically and reflectively, and respond ethically during group discussion
- Use technology to communicate and acquire information

Learning Goals for English 1301

- Develop cross-cultural understanding and respect
- Use writing, reading, and academic inquiry for learning, critical thinking, and problem solving
- Write, read, and speak for a variety of real-world purposes and for various audiences
- Write with readers in mind
- Read with writers in mind
- Deepen understanding of the reflexive processes of invention, drafting, revision, and editing
- Connect concepts across learning community courses
- Learn, evaluate, and use computer technology as a writing, reading, and research tool

Learning Goals for English 1302

- Develop cross-cultural understanding and respect

- Use writing, reading, and academic inquiry to critically engage increasingly complex open-ended questions and ill-defined problems
- Write, read, and speak for a variety of real-world purposes and for various audiences
- Write with readers in mind
- Read with writers in mind
- Integrate knowledge from learning community courses
- Learn, evaluate, and use computer technology as a writing, reading, and research tool

English 1301 Course Objectives

- Read texts that enhance cross-cultural understanding and respect
- Analyze a variety of texts written for various rhetorical purposes and audiences
- Evaluate a variety of texts as ethically responsible and rhetorically effective
- Understand the relationship between disciplinary perspectives and criteria for validity and rhetorical effectiveness
- Connect ideas, claims and issues across contexts
- Understand the nature of inquiry
- Locate appropriate primary and secondary sources [emphasize personal experience, readings and qualitative research observations and interviews]
- Evaluate appropriate primary and secondary sources in terms of credibility, context, author, purpose and audience
- Extend strategies for invention, revision, and the production of texts to academic discourse [emphasize focus, audience, organizational strategies, and the constraints of in-class timed writings]
- Integrate quotations and supporting material from experience, readings, and research
- Use conventions that are rhetorically appropriate to the purpose of the texts [emphasize sentence boundaries, non-sexist usage, editing for clarity and style]
- Develop a vocabulary and context-specific criteria for assessing their own writing and their peers
- Collaborate and interact with peers and instructors for various purposes through discussions, peer critique, interchanges, on-line exchanges, workshops, and conferences
- Understand the limits, problems, and possibilities connected with computer technology
- Use computer technology to generate texts, discuss readings, communicate across disciplinary contexts, and solve problems
- Generate a writing portfolio
- Self-assess inquiry, writing processes and products

English 1302 Objectives

- Explore diverse perspectives on learning community issues
- Analyze and evaluate diverse arguments for ethical and rhetorical effectivenes
- Investigate the nature of research processes
- Locate appropriate primary and secondary sources [emphasize print and digital sources]
- Evaluate appropriate primary and secondary sources in terms of credibility, context, author, purpose and audience
- Construct arguments that are ethically responsible and rhetorically effective
- Work with multiple modes of argumentation
- Synthesize appropriate primary and secondary sources

- Use conventions of documentation appropriate to the purpose of the text
- Collaborate and interact with peers and instructors for various purposes through discussions, peer critique, interchanges, on-line exchanges, workshops, and conferences
- Use computer technology to generate texts, discuss readings, locate and recover research materials, and communicate across disciplinary contexts
- Generate a research portfolio
- Self-assess research process and product

English 1301 Learning Outcomes

Students will be able to

- Analyze and interpret a variety of texts
- Write in several genres
- Produce an introduction with a solid focus, direction, and purpose
- Integrate internal citations into the writer's ideas
- Connect ideas across courses

English 1302 Learning Outcomes

Students will be able to

- Identify position, claims, and evidence in arguments
- Evaluate position, claims, and evidence in arguments
- Construct arguments on more than one side of an issue
- Produce an introduction with a solid focus, direction, and purpose
- Integrate internal citations into the writer's ideas
- Integrate a citation system that is identifiable, functional, and consistent
- Connect ideas across disciplines

Credit by Exam

Refer to the University Catalog for details regarding transfer of credit for core courses, including English 1301 and 1302.

CLEP and AP Exams

CLEP	Minimum Score	A&M-Corpus Christi	Credit Hours
	Required	Courses(s)	Awarded
Freshman College Composition** with required essay	50	ENGL 1301, ENGL 1302	0-3-6

***Depending on the quality of the essay, students will be awarded 0, 3, or 6 hours of credit for the Freshman College Composition exam. Credit may be awarded for ENGL 1301, or for both ENGL 1301 and ENGL 1302.*

AP Examination	Minimum Score	A&M-Corpus Christi	Credit Hours
	Required	Courses(s)	Awarded
English, Language and Composition	4	ENGL 1301	3
or			
English, Literature and Composition	4	ENGL 1301	3

Where are we?

The First Year Programs Office is located in Faculty Center, office 253. All the Seminar Leaders and Composition instructors have drop-off crates, mailboxes, and offices in this space. Office hours and email addresses are posted on the door.

FACULTY CENTER IS BUILDING 8 ON THE CAMPUS MAP BELOW.

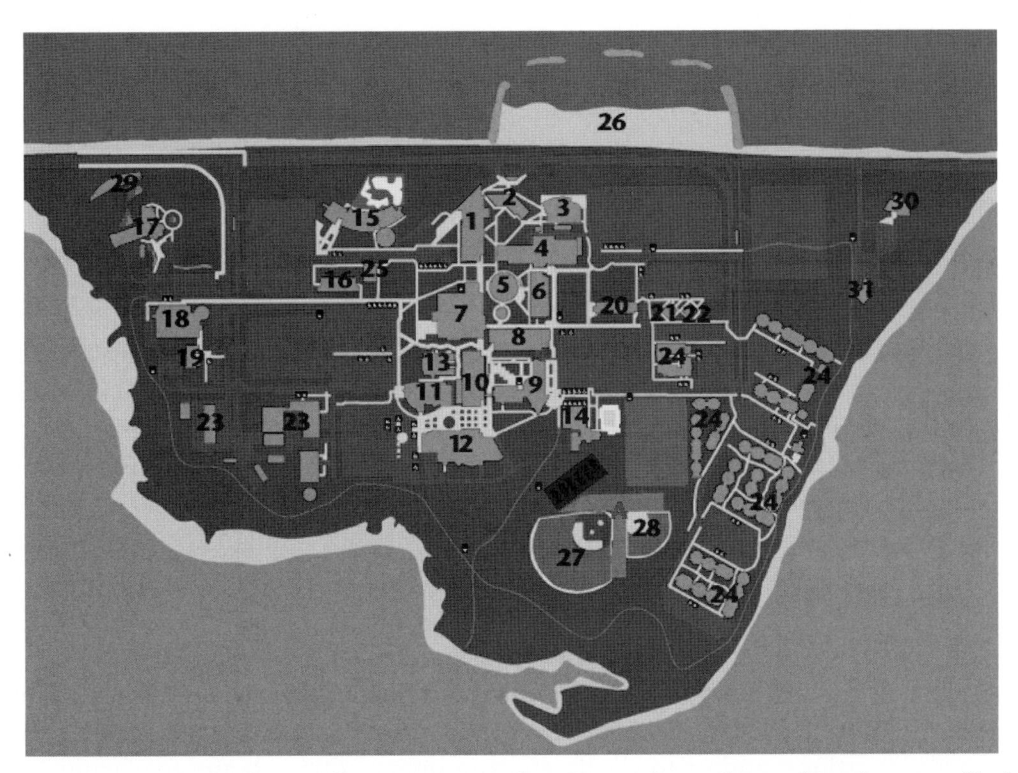

To most easily find our office, enter Faculty Center from the parking lot or walk through the first-floor atrium to the parking lot end of the building. You will see a stairwell to the left of the glass exit doors. Go up to the second floor. On your immediate left will be a door that leads into our office space. Do not hesitate to come in!

If you need elevator access, you must enter the building from the end closest to the library, take the elevator to the second floor, proceed through the doors marked "College of Liberal Arts," and follow the hallway back down the entire length of the building to our office. It requires a sharp left-hand turn in front of bookcases, and a right-hand turn by the refrigerator/microwave. You may ask any administrative assistant or faculty member along the hallway where the First-Year Programs office is located, and they will assist you.

First Year Learning Communities Staff

Office: FC 253
Phone: (361) 825-2150

Sara Chapa
Administrative Assistant
sara.chapa@tamucc.edu

Susan Wolff Murphy
University Core Curriculum Program Co-Director
FYWP Coordinator
susan.murphy@tamucc.edu

Juan Carlos Huerta
University Core Curriculum Program Co-Director
juan.huerta@tamucc.edu

Rita Sperry
Seminar Coordinator
rita.sperry@tamucc.edu

Steve Schwerin
Program Coordinator II
steven.schwerin@tamucc.edu

Ms. Sara Chapa is our administrative assistant and will be happy to help you with any questions you have. **Mr. Steve Schwerin** is our Program Coordinator. He can register students for online courses, help solve scheduling issues, and answer questions. **Dr. Susan Wolff Murphy** is our Director. She can answer questions and listen to feedback and/or complaints regarding our program. **Ms. Rita Sperry** coordinates seminar, and will be happy to discuss the purpose and structure of seminar with any student.

Office Hours

All faculty are required to post hours when they are available to talk to students outside of class. Office hours are excellent opportunities to communicate privately with an instructor, to ask questions, and/or to clarify an assignment. Office hours for faculty in the FYLCP are posted on our office door (FC 253) and online, at the FYLCP website at: http://firstyear.tamucc.edu/wiki

Contact/Find Your Teacher

All Seminar Instructors and Composition instructors have offices in FC 253. The best way to contact them is email. They have emails and office hours posted on their course pages available on the FYLCP website at: http://firstyear.tamucc.edu/wiki, or you can phone 825-2150 for this information.

CHAPTER 2

Academic Writing

Writers in the university, meaning students, faculty, administrators, and staff, must operate within the boundaries and expectations of what is appropriate, ethical, and responsible. Just as writers in all contexts do, they make choices about the subjects, words, and structures they use as they write. As writers, members of the university participate in various discourse communities. This chapter will help you see how academic writing is an extension of writing you have done previously, and how you will be expected to grow as a writer, by explaining the ways that the act of writing is an exercise of a network of types of knowledge:

- discourse communities
- genres
- writing process
- rhetorical situation
- subject matter (Beaufort, 2007).

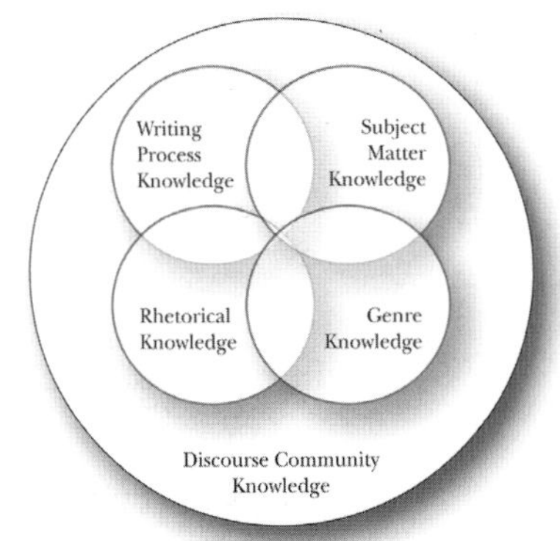

Discourse Communities

Have you ever been at a party and gotten into a group of people talking about things you don't understand? It could be related to a sport you don't like or a career you are not in. The words, the jokes, and the values expressed don't necessarily make any sense. You might listen with a half-smile on your face until you can escape to get more food or decide it is time to go home early.

However, you might cross the room, join another cluster of speakers, and find yourself completely at home. Maybe you find co-workers, best friends, teammates, or family members. Suddenly, the jokes, vocabulary, and values all seem familiar and comfortable.

This is an example of being in a discourse community. A discourse community is any group of people who use similar ways of speaking to express their belonging to a group. Discourse communities can be defined by a job, by education, by ethnicity, by age, by movies or sports people follow, or by the myriad set of possibilities that define our identities.

When you are within your most intimate discourse communities, you feel comfortable and confident. You are secure in your ways of speaking and writing. You are the expert. When you are in a discourse community of which you are not a member, you may feel lost, confused, and dislocated.

Being lost in an unfamiliar discourse community, or being a "fish out of water," is often a trick used by Hollywood to create comedy. It is a situation that most people have experienced to a lesser or greater degree at some point in their lives, and it works well if the audience understands more about the community than the lost character does.

As a first year student, you might be a "fish out of water." You are entering the discourse community of the university. In fact, you are joining a convergence of many overlapping disciplinary and professional disciplines, all united for the purpose of acculturating new members by educating students in their ways of speaking, thinking, and writing.

As you move from course to course, major to major, college to college, and professor to professor, you will see differences in lexicon (vocabulary), jargon, practices of thinking and researching, and ways of writing and presenting information. As the traveler, you will have to adjust to each new discourse community in order to be successful in your college career.

Don't fret. You are already an expert at crossing boundaries between discourse communities. First, you lived at home, a combination of people and places that defined your accent, your ideas of what is "normal," your language, and many other features of your identity.

Then, you began school. You interacted with teachers and friends. People who came from different homes and belief systems. Folks who might have talked differently. New rules of behavior and language.

You might have immigrated to another country. Or traveled for school. Or traveled as an "Army Brat." You might have gotten a job, or many jobs. You might have lived with different members of your family. Each time, you have adjusted, added new elements to your facility with language, new ways of speaking, thinking, and operating in the world.

So you are an expert at moving between discourse communities. Now, when you write, you will be expected to think about what discourse community you're operating within. What rules or expectations do they have for writing?

Discourse communities use writing for many different purposes, to a variety of audiences, and in many genres. These are all interrelated. In real life, writers' purposes and audiences decide the genres they create, and their ability to recognize these constraints and make appropriate choices determines their success.

Genres

Genre is defined as, "a class or category of artistic endeavor having a particular form, content, technique, or the like: *the genre of epic poetry; the genre of symphonic music*" (Dictionary.com). In simpler terms, genre means type or kind.

Discourse communities define the genres of writing that are appropriate for various tasks completed within or by that community. Genres of writing include novels, poetry, and plays, but they also include reports, feature stories, memoirs, and instruction manuals. Within each of these genres are subgenres: the romance novel, the mystery novel, or the science fiction novel. The sonnet, the haiku, or the epic.

Due to the fact that a genre is defined by the discourse community that creates it, there is no one measure of "good writing."

Likewise, there is not one formula for a research paper, in spite of the fact that many professors and classes will assign that genre. A historian will expect a different version of that genre than a sociologist will.

As a writer, it is your job to figure out how to successfully create these different genres of writing. In First Year Composition, it is our job to help you develop your ability to recognize the rules of genres, to move between various discourse communities and sets of expectations, and to become a successful writer on your own terms.

Writing Process

The act of writing is comprised of several recursive, overlapping steps. "Step" is a misnomer because the word implies a set order, logically followed, that leads to a certain end. However, aspects of the writing process can be repeated or skipped. These steps are often abbreviated or extended, used or ignored by the expert writer, depending on the task at hand.

When tackling a new or difficult writing task, it is important to not underestimate the value of various aspects of the writing process. It may be beneficial to try ones you have previously rejected or to modify your routine. Be open minded and experiment.

Aspect One: Invention

Invention, otherwise known as brainstorming, is the process of generating ideas. Under various guises, invention is the first, and sometimes most important, step of the writing process. It is also the most creative and the most individualized. Invention is comprised of various strategies and methods: freewriting, clustering, bubbling, outlining, and journaling, among many others, are all methods of generating ideas.

Aspect Two: Drafting

Once writers define their task or once they transition from writing without a specific goal to writing for a purpose, they could be said to enter the stage of the writing process generally referred to as drating. Drafting can also be said to be a time to refine your thoughts. As writer E. M. Forster wrote, "How can I know what I think till I see what I say?" Sometimes we are not clear about what we are saying until we write it out, so in many ways, drafting is also invention.

Aspect Three: Revising

As writers draft, they re-read what they have written. Sometimes writers re-read because they have taken a break, and they have to figure out what they've done before. Sometimes they're stuck, and writers re-read to generate new ideas. Re-reading allows writers to see again, or to review, or to re-vision their message. Revision involves stepping back from creating to assess, to organize, and/or to mix things up. Revision is messy and usually occurs several times during the drafting process. It may lead back to invention, or it may lead toward editing.

Many professional writers use fellow writers as critical readers for their writing during the revising process because having a real audience allows writers to see and hear how their writing is being read, interpreted, and reacted to. Writers can only imagine the audience's reaction so well. Our biases and experiences get in the way. Having an actual audience read your work and respond to it can be one of the most valuable steps in the writing process. University students will ask friends, family members, classmates, instructors, and/or writing center consultants to help them with revision. The more familiar a reader is with your genre, discourse community, and purpose, the better they will be able to respond appropriately and constructively to your drafting.

Aspect Four: Editing

Writers edit when they are finished drafting and revising. When a piece of writing is as good as it is going to get, writers will "clean it up." Meaning, they will read it critically for the expectations of the genre: appropriate spelling, word choice, use of technical terms (jargon), mechanics, grammar, and documentation of sources. Manuscript guidelines will be followed. An editor's job is to make sure every aspect of the piece of writing is correct for the purpose and audience for which it is intended.

Aspect Five: Publication

When your writing is published, it is shared with an audience. This step can take various forms, from being printed and sold, performed by a "company of players," read as a guide, or presented at a conference. Much writing for school does not reach any audience other than your professor for the purposes of a grade. However, the First Year Writing Program does host an event each semester to allow students to publish more broadly (*Celebration Day* in Fall and *First-Year Research Conference* in Spring). Additionally, there are undergraduate research opportunities, *The Windward Journal*, and the Haas Writing Awards.

Writing process strategies will be discussed in Chapters Three, Four, and Five.

Rhetorical Situation

The different parts of the rhetorical situation will be discussed in Chapter Six and Chapter Seven.

Subject Matter

The topics you will write about will vary from those of your peers. You may foray into the disciplines of criminal justice, sociology, political science, or history. You will be responsible for researching your topics to learn about the subject matter you will be writing, and using appropriate forms of evidence for those fields or subjects. Research and documentation will be the primary means of learning about your subject matter; these strategies are discussed in Chapter Eight.

CHAPTER 3

Brainstorming, Outlining, and Drafting

What Is Brainstorming?

We write best when we write about topics we are interested in and are familiar with. Writing is like painting in that it is a very individualized process. Someone can show us how to apply paint to a canvas, but eventually, we must make these acts our own by adding our own touches to them.

You can come up with ideas for essays in many ways; however, if you are stuck and cannot find a topic to use, brainstorming, as part of the pre-writing you do, can help narrow down general ideas into a focused topic and then help you decide what to use as supporting detail. You may already have your own style of pre-writing; however, experiment with different methods of brainstorming to find what best suits your style.

Freewriting

You should think of freewriting as a "no holds barred" type of brainstorming. When you freewrite, begin by allotting yourself a specific amount of time, such as ten to fifteen minutes. This technique is more constructive when you already have an idea for your topic. However, freewriting can be used to generate ideas for topics. Begin by simply writing. Write whatever comes into your mind. Do not be concerned with punctuation, grammar, or complete sentences. Use symbols or question marks in place of words that you cannot come up with automatically. If you cannot think of anything to write, simply jot down the phrase "I don't know" until you begin writing other words. Remember, this does not have to make sense to anyone else. This should be as stress-free as possible.

Here is an example done in three minutes with the topic of "peace."

I only have three minutes to come up with something decent to write about. This is stupid. This is not peaceful this is stressful. <u>Peace</u> is not writing under pressure. Peace is <u>being barefoot on grass by a lake or hearing people laugh.</u> Besides, who can think of peace with all of the <u>atrocities</u> in the world? Peace is <u>not war.</u> Peace is the <u>absence of war</u>, but maybe it is more than what it isn't. Peace is represented by <u>doves, white flags, smiles, and happiness.</u> But I guess peace doesn't have to be related to war. It can be associated with <u>one's mindset, one's life,</u> or anything that we come into contact with in our daily lives.

Once your time is up, sit back, and look at what you have written. Separate out the promising phrases, organize these ideas, and then expand them.

Go back, and read your paragraph again, underlining potential topics and subtopics.

Looping

Looping is a variation of freewriting. It can be a more constructive brainstorming exercise for those who need a little more focus than freewriting provides. This technique works best when you already have a general topic in mind.

For example, you have been assigned to write on your definition of war. Take out several sheets of paper and begin to freewrite as defined earlier. When time is up, read over what you have written, and try to pinpoint a central idea that has emerged from what you have written. Perhaps it is the idea that you liked best for whatever reason. It must simply be an idea that stands out to you. Put this thought or idea in one sentence below the freewriting. This is called your "center of gravity" statement. This completes loop number one.

To begin loop number two, begin freewriting from the previous "center of gravity" statement. Freewrite for another ten minutes. Upon completion of this freewriting session, you will once again assess what you have written and extract a compelling or important idea that emerged from your writing. Write this main idea below your freewriting. This is your second "center of gravity" statement. You will begin freewriting from the second center of gravity statement.

Example:

Loop Number 1:

War is chaos, fighting, and mental anguish. Our traditional definition of war encompasses historical "wars" such as the Revolutionary war, the Civil War, World War I, World War II, and Vietnam just to name a few. War has been a massive part of societies for centuries. War is death, destruction, and bombing. However, I don't think war has to be defined in terms of actual countries physically fighting one another. Wars are waged everyday in people's hearts, minds, and lives.

Loop Number 2:

Wars are waged everyday in people's hearts, minds, and lives. The definition of war exceeds beyond the boundaries of our usual definition. War is loneliness, heartbreak, mental illness, daily adversity, and struggles. We normally think of war as having heroes and fantastic stories of bravery. However, if war is defined as doing battle against a foe that is challenging one's established way of life, then loneliness, heartbreak, mental illness, disease, adversity, and struggles can fit easily within the definition of war.

You should continue this looping process until you are satisfied and comfortable with the topic you have generated.

Journaling

Sometimes, instructors will lead you toward a topic by assigning journals. These are informal writings that allow you to take a vague idea and write about it. These journals allow you to follow an idea or a hunch without worrying about penalty. Think of these journals as a more controlled version of freewriting. Once you complete a journal entry, you can set it aside for a time and come back to it at a later date when you are rested and ready to approach the topic once again. You may even have new ideas or a different take than you initially had.

Example:

Journal Assignment: Write your initial impressions of Faulkner's "A Rose for Emily."

When I read Faulkner's "A Rose for Emily," I was initially appalled. Miss Emily is clearly sick as she murdered Homer Baron and kept his body in the upper room locked away from the rest of the world. However, I was looking through a scrapbook today and was shocked at what I found. There, in that scrapbook were pressed flowers, pictures, ticket stubs, and other mementos. Only then did it occur to me that I was acting as Miss Emily had acted. I saved mementos and pictures of a special time that would otherwise be lost forever with nothing to show for it but a memory. I was, just as Miss Emily did, capturing a moment. I suppose it should be noted that Miss Emily had suffered some tragic events in her life and did not have the proper outlets by which to express her heartbreak and loneliness. She merely acts in the only manner she finds effective. In this respect, Faulkner's story demonstrates Miss Emily as a profoundly sympathetic character.

From this journal, you can revisit this topic after possibly utilizing other brainstorming exercises or even after discussion with your instructor and other classmates.

Clustering or Mapping

Another technique you can use for brainstorming is clustering, sometimes referred to as mapping. You can cluster in two different ways.

- Start with possible topic ideas; then cluster them by drawing circles around them and organizing them into clusters.
- Start with a clustering grid, and then fill in the circles with ideas.

Whatever way you decide to cluster, start by putting your general topic in the middle of a blank page. If you want to use the first clustering method, jot down possible subtopics and details all around the central circle. After you have written down as many subtopics or details as you can, locate the more general subtopics, circle them, and attach these circles to the middle circle that holds the general topic. After this, find details that will support the subtopics, circle them, and attach these circles to the subtopic circles. When you have circled enough subtopics and details to start outlining or writing your paper, erase or cross out all the extra, unconnected information.

If you want to try the second clustering method, write your general topic in the middle of a blank page, and draw lines from this circle to five or six circles (these will hold your subtopics). Then, draw lines from the subtopic circles to three or four other circles (these will be your supporting details). Regardless of the clustering method you choose, you should allot between ten and twenty minutes for this brainstorming process. What you end up with might look something like this cluster/map that uses the movie *Fight Club* as the general topic.

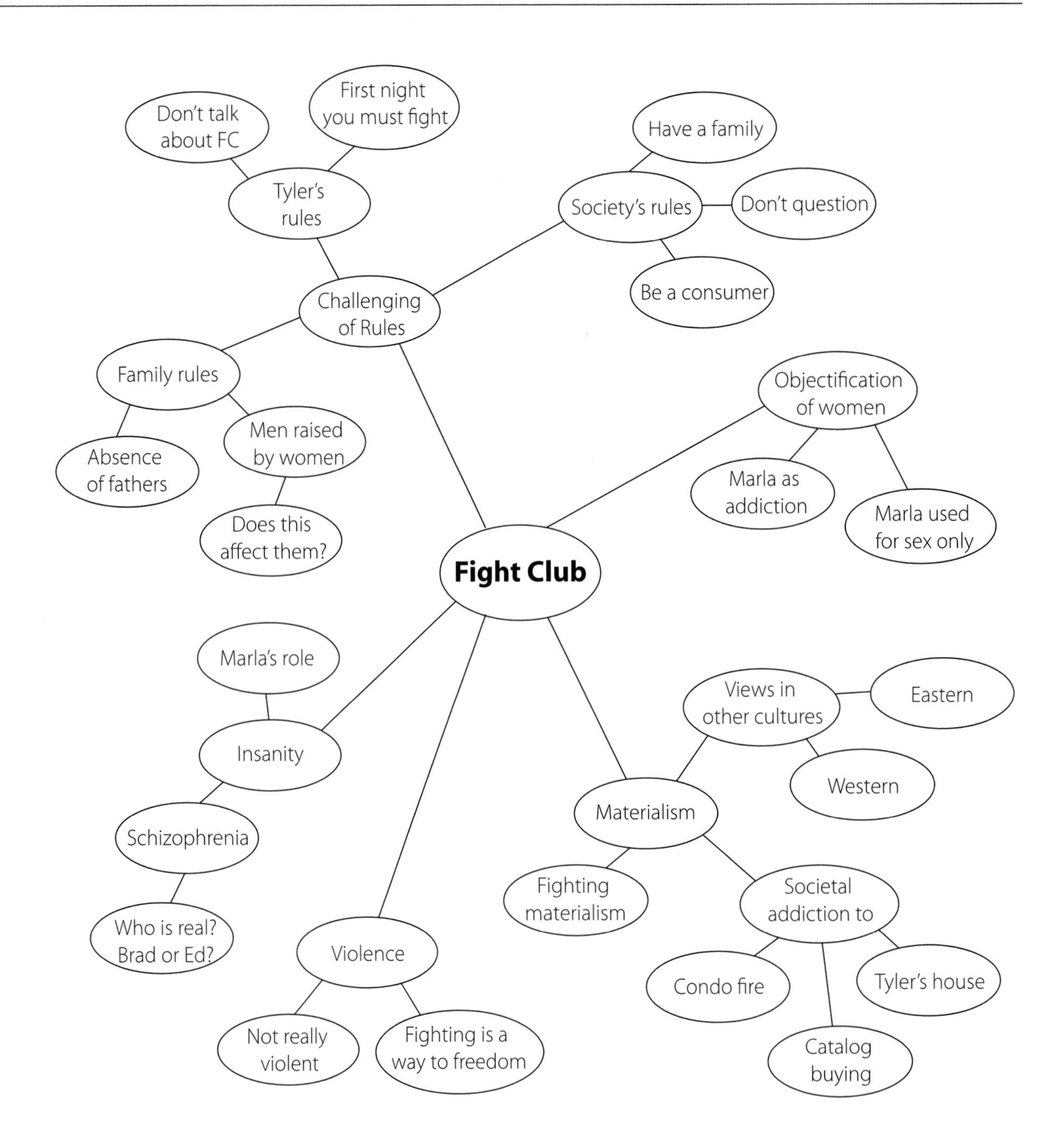

Cubing

Yet another way to generate ideas is cubing. Imagine a cube with six sides, or use a die from a game set you have around your house. Next, imagine the numbers for the commands given below are written on each side of the cube, or attach the commands to the sides of a die. Picture yourself rolling the cube (or roll the actual die), and write following the commands that come up.

Listed below are the commands you should visualize on your cube.

- **Describe it:** What does the subject look like? Sound like? Engage all five senses if possible.
- **Compare and contrast it:** What is the subject similar to? What is it different from? How so?

- **Free associate with it:** What does the subject remind you of? Any particular memories?
- **Analyze it:** How does it work? What is its significance?
- **Argue for or against it:** What advantages and disadvantages does it have?
- **Apply it:** What are the uses of your subject? What can you do with it?

Write whatever comes to your mind for ten minutes or so. When you have finished cubing, take the topics and subtopics you have generated and organize them by clustering or outlining them.

Listing

Another way to brainstorm is to simply jot down any ideas that pop into your head for about ten minutes. After you have finished your list, look for connections between ideas, or look for one main idea that encompasses several small ones.

Here is an example for the general topic of **television**.

Entertaining	Usually thirty minute programs
Informative	Media
Corrupting	Listen
Poisoning	Corporate sponsorship
News	Music Television
Comedy	Home shopping
Drama	"boob tube"
Sports	Game shows
Educational	Remote control
Biased	mind-numbing
Commercials	Weight gain
People	possible contributor to "dumbing down" of society

After examining the list, do you make any connections? Does anything stand out that you might want to write about? If so, try clustering or outlining the idea to see if it can be developed.

Interviewing and Discussing

Sometimes we have an idea that is unclear in our minds. However, once we begin talking about this topic with others, our idea becomes clearer, or the other person may be able to offer a perspective that you had not thought of previously.

As you are discussing your idea with a classmate or a friend, allow yourself to think of the subject as your friend or classmate asks you questions about your subject that would naturally come up in conversation. Also, your "interviewer" might ask you what are termed "Journalism questions," such as

- Who? Who believes X? Who is involved?
- When? When did it happen? When did you change?
- Why? Why did X do Y? Why is this interesting?
- What? What happened? What did you do?
- Where? Where did it happen? Where were you?
- How? How did you become involved? How is it interesting?

Make sure you listen to what you are saying as you are being "interviewed." Was there a particular part of the subject that you were most interested in talking about? If so, why? You may find that you have discussed your way into an interesting topic. However, this may not prove fruitful. If you are still without a clear subject by the end of the "interview" session, ask your classmate or friend questions. If they had to write an essay based on the information you had just discussed, what would they write about? Why?

Questioning

Sometimes no one is available for interviewing. If this type of brainstorming works best for you, try questioning yourself about the subject. Think of your favorite attorney on television or in books. How would he or she cross examine a witness? You should model your cross examination of yourself in this manner. You could ask yourself a million questions about your subject. However, below is a list of five categories to help you start narrowing your subject.

- Definition: How does the dictionary define the word or subject? How does the majority define it? What is its history? Where did it come from? Give some examples.
- Compare and contrast: What is it similar to? What is it different than? Think also along the lines of synonyms and antonyms or opposites.
- Relationship: What are its causes and effects?
- Circumstance: Is it possible or impossible? When has it happened before? Are there any ways to prevent it?
- Testimony: What do people say about it? What has been written about it? Have you had any experience with it? Has any relevant research been done on the subject?

Outlining

Outlining can help you brainstorm for subtopics, or it can be used as a method for organizing the material that other brainstorming techniques have helped you generate. Either way, the value of the outline is its ability to help you to plan, to see logical connections between your ideas, and to see obvious places to add new ideas and details.

An informal outline can be just a map of paragraphs that you plan to use. For example, here is a short, informal outline for the topic of **effective study practices**.

Body paragraph one: discussion of free services

Body paragraph two: discussion of writing assistants

Body paragraph three: discussion of learning aids

You can also add examples and supporting details and construct a more detailed informal outline.

I. Free services

    A. Minicourse on improving study skills

    B. Writing assistants

        a. composition

        b. foreign language

    C. Weekly Seminars

        a. stress management

        b. test anxiety

II. Writing assistants

    A. Top graduate students in their field

    B. Experienced teachers

III. Learning aids

    A. Supplemental texts

    B. Workbooks

Note that the above is not a formal outline, which would have strictly parallel parts and would be expressed in complete sentences. Unless your instructor requests a formal outline, do not feel you must construct one. An informal or working outline helps you get to the drafting stage, but it should not restrict you from changing subtopics or details to make your essay topic stronger.

CHAPTER 4

Revision

What Is Revision?

Revision literally means "to see or look at again," and this is what you do when you revise your writing. Revision and editing are two different parts of the writing process, but they are often grouped together and referred to as rewriting, revision, redrafting, editing, or proofreading. However, revision is one of the creative parts of the writing process, rather than a time to correct your grammar.

Revision is what writing specialists consider the **global** process of redrafting, and global characteristics of writing focus on overall issues, such as the following.

- Content
- Thesis
- Organization
- Word choice
- Word use

Often, writers try to revise and edit at the same time; however, this is not a good idea. When you edit, focus on what writing specialists call **local** issues of editing, such as the following.

- Grammar
- Sentence variety
- Mechanics
- Spelling
- Formatting

This focused attention to minute parts of words and sentences often distracts a writer from thoroughly developing ideas. Thus, instructors and skilled writers recommend that any writer try to separate revision and editing into two activities. In many freshman composition classes, instructors purposely divide revision from editing by using separate peer workshop days and by giving different grades or grade percentages for these activities as part of an overall paper grade.

Why do you need to revise?

Writers who revise often discover and develop new or better ideas through the revision process. Revision is changing the paper, hopefully for the better. Most professional or skilled writers view revision as a necessary part of their writing because it is useful for generating new ideas, focusing and reorganizing ideas, and polishing the overall paper. A draft is a work in progress, and it's a good idea to write multiple drafts for each essay in order to write the best paper and get the best grade possible.

What types of changes can you make?

You can **add**, **delete**, and **substitute** material during the revision process. For example, if a sentence is unclear, you can add information to clarify your point, delete ambiguous words or phrases, or substitute a new sentence that has more clarity.

How can you use technology to help you revise?

Microsoft Word has two features that are particularly helpful when revising and editing: the **Comment** Feature and the **Track Changes** Feature.

You might want to ask a question, make an observation, or suggest a change, but not want to actually revise the author's paper. In this case, use the Comment Feature. In order to add a comment that will appear in the margin in a box, follow these steps:

1. Highlight the portion of the text to be associated with a comment.
2. Go to Insert on the toolbar and select Comment.
3. Each reviewer's comments will be labeled differently and show on the screen in different colors.

If you want to actually revise a person's paper but to show that it has been changed, you can use Track Changes. This might be appropriate if you see a mechanical or grammatical error that is hard to explain, but easy to fix. You can show the author your fix at the same time that you can show them the error by using Track Changes.

1. On the toolbar, select "Tools," and select "Highlight Changes"
2. Any changes you make will be done in color.
3. To turn it off, go back to "Highlight Changes" and unclick the appropriate boxes.

In both of these cases, you can suggest revisions and edits without erasing or deleting the original text. That way if the author disagrees with you, he or she can choose to ignore your feedback. Or if the author agrees with you, she or he might appreciate the guidance you have provided. And all this work is saved electronically so you can turn it in to your instructor as evidence of drafting, revising, and editing.

What Are the Different Levels of Revision?

When you revise, you focus on **content**, **organization**, and **word choice**. However, each of these global issues can be found on different levels of your essay. Be sure to revise on all levels: the **overall essay**, **paragraphs**, **sentences**, and **words**. It's best to divide these levels of revision and work on them separately since a good revision plan includes investigation of all these levels.

What should you focus on when revising at the essay level?

When you revise at the essay level, focus on large-scale changes that will improve the overall essay. Here is a list of essay-level concerns that you should consider each time you write and revise an essay.

- Look first at the central idea of the essay. If **all** sentences in the essay do not support this main idea, you will need to either revise the main idea or revise the support in the essay. Although it is not necessary to have an explicit thesis statement, it is a good idea to include one in a college essay, so you have a clearly defined central idea that will help you write the essay and help guide your reader through the essay.

- Make sure that you have an audience in mind when writing and revising the essay. If a reader cannot see himself or herself as the audience, then you need to revise and pay more attention to the audience of the essay.
- Check the introduction and the rest of the essay for your underlying purpose in writing the essay. If any of the support given throughout the essay does not support your purpose, you will need to revise the support.
- Review the overall organization of the essay. Does each body paragraph support the central idea of the essay? Are the paragraphs ordered in a way that will make sense to the reader?
- Check the balance inside the essay. Are any of the supporting paragraphs out of balance with the rest of the essay? If so, check whether or not large paragraphs can be split or short paragraphs can be reorganized together.
- Make sure that your essay flows well. Use transitions between body paragraphs, so your reader will not get confused when you change topics.
- Review your central idea if it is an argument, making sure that you have addressed counterarguments at some point in the essay.
- Be sure to use an interesting title that will encourage your reader to take the time to read your essay.

What should you focus on when revising at the paragraph level?

After revising on the essay level, you need to check whether the paragraphs in your essay are effective. Here is a list of paragraph-level concerns that you should consider each time you write and revise an essay.

- Reread the introductory paragraph. Does it include an effective lead-in to the central idea? Will the introductory material capture your reader's interest? Be sure to stay away from overused introductory strategies, such as providing a dictionary definition or general statements like *today's society.*
- Focus on topic sentences. Read only the first sentences of each paragraph in order; does this give a good indication about the central idea of the essay and the supporting evidence?
- Add more examples and details to weakly-developed paragraphs. Stay away from only giving generalizations. For example, instead of saying, *Nurses are not easy to find*, say *In 2003, Tennessee is experiencing a shortage of 154,000 nurses*, and cite the source of the information.
- Check summarized, paraphrased, or quoted material that you use for support.
- Check for coherence within body paragraphs. If you provide multiple supporting sentences, use transitions to join them together. Review and perhaps rewrite the introduction and conclusion.
- Reread your concluding paragraph. In addition to reinforcing key ideas from the body of the essay, try to end in a way that makes your reader want to read more. Without introducing new information, making a prediction or inviting a response works well.

What should you focus on when revising at the sentence level?

Writers often check for sentence grammar and punctuation and forget to check for sentence-level changes that would clarify content or organization. Here are some sentence-level strategies to use when you revise your essays.

- Check for sentence clarity. Does each sentence make sense? Check for ambiguity. For instance, a sentence such as *Visiting relatives can be bothersome* has multiple meanings and needs clarification. Changing this sentence to *My relatives who visit often can be bothersome* or *I do not like to visit relatives* will clear up the ambiguity.
- Try not to use long introductory phrases or clauses. These usually distract the reader from what you are trying to emphasize in the sentence. A sentence such as *Before I left for work that day and caught the bus on the corner of Main Street and Jones Boulevard, I broke my leg in the shower* has a long unnecessary introductory clause that de-emphasizes the main point of the sentence.
- Use sentence-combining techniques to provide more sentence variety in the essay. Readers get bored reading the same structure over and over again. Balancing short, simple sentences with compound or complex sentences works best.

What should you focus on when revising at the word level?

Choosing your words well helps your reader understand the central point more easily. Revising word-level problems will improve not only the content of your essay, but it will also improve the way the paper flows. Here are some word-level strategies you can use when revising your essay.

- Look for wordiness. Cut empty phrases, such as *there are, it is, I feel that, I know that, you will understand that, I think, in today's society.*
- Use concrete nouns for subjects, and avoid overusing pronouns, especially at the beginning of sentences.
- Ask your instructor about his or her policy on using first person (*I, me, my*) and second person (*you, your, yours*).
- Be sure to use *you* appropriately if you use it. *You* can only be used if the reader is actually the *you* referent.
- Change passive verbs to active ones when possible.
- Read aloud for unnecessary repetition. Replace overused words with synonyms, but be careful that you clearly understand how to use words you borrow from a thesaurus.
- Check the tone of your essay since word choice plays a role in creating the overall tone. If your instructor asks you to use academic tone, do not use conversational-type word choices, such as *Well, I then went to the bus stop on the corner and then got on the bus and then took it downtown* or *I was chillin' in my crib.*
- Review transition use throughout the essay. Pay particular attention to using transitions between body paragraphs and within body paragraphs when switching from one supporting point to another.

WHAT ARE TEN STEPS TO HELP YOU REVISE?

1. Put aside your rough or first draft for a time before you start your revision.
2. Print out your draft, and read it slowly, making notes as you go.
3. Revise on the essay level.
4. Revise on the paragraph level.
5. Revise on the sentence level.
6. Revise on the word level.
7. Ask someone to read your essay for revision purposes only. It is best to find someone who understands the difference between revision and editing and who will only comment on global concerns.
8. Incorporate changes from #7.
9. Participate in a peer-revision workshop in class if available.
10. Incorporate changes from #9, and then begin the editing stage.

Who Can Help You Revise?

The person most invested in helping you revise is **YOU**. Be sure to include enough time for a thorough revision in your writing process, and focus on the essay, paragraph, sentence, and word levels one at a time.

Next, find **someone else** who is in your class or who is taking First Year Composition with the same instructor since this person is the most familiar with the assignment requirements. You can also ask your roommate, friend, work colleague, or family member to help you revise; however, these revisers will probably need instruction in what revision really is. It will not help you if they focus on editing when you need to be focusing on revision. In addition, be careful not to have anyone rewrite your words or write sections of your paper. Your reviewers need to make suggestions, but you are the **only** one who should put those suggestions to paper since having someone else rewrite your words is a type of plagiarism.

The best way to find people to help you revise is to participate fully in your **peer revision workshop**. Finish a rough draft of your paper, and revise it thoroughly yourself. Then, bring this revised draft to your class revision workshop. Incorporate any changes that your peer suggests if the change improves your paper.

The **Writing Center** provides assistance for the revision level. Be clear with the Writing Consultant what your assignment is, and be sure to incorporate those suggestions that you feel will improve your essay.

You can also ask your **instructor** for revision help during his or her office hours. Be sure to have specific questions ready; have a list of things that you found difficult to revise when you did your thorough revision. Some instructors allow students to submit papers electronically for revision help; however, before you do this, check with your instructor about his or her policy on this. Most instructors like to have you and your paper present when they discuss possible global changes to the paper.

Why should you consider using peer revision?

Peer revision, whether it is inside or outside class, gives you a chance to hear from an immediate audience, rather than from an instructor. This mid-step allows you to improve your paper without negatively impacting your grade, and when you exchange papers with someone else, it is usually a win-win situation. Getting immediate feedback is also a plus since using this strategy will help you develop your essay more before it gets turned in for evaluation.

Working with other writers can also help boost your confidence about an essay. If your peer reader enjoys your essay and gives you good advice, you feel better about the essay, and in turn, will probably work more on it. In addition, peer workshops allow you to see firsthand that other writers also struggle with the same things you do; most first drafts are less than excellent essays, and you will feel better about your own in-process essay by being aware of this.

Peer revision, most importantly, gets you into the habit of working collaboratively, something you will do in other classes and in the workplace after you leave the freshman writing classroom.

How Can Peer Revision Work Most Effectively?

When you ask for revision help, you often need to give feedback in return on your peer's work. Sometimes, it is difficult for students to participate in peer revision; it takes time to get used to incorporating this step into the writing process. Here are some good strategies to use when participating in peer revision.

- Get over your shyness about sharing your work with others. Understand that all writers are in the same boat when it comes to sharing their work; it is difficult to let others see a work in progress, but sharing your writing and receiving feedback improves your writing.
- Be an interested reader, and give meaningful comments and critiques.
- Use peer revision forms to help you give advice. Answer all the questions on the forms with full answers that will help the writer revise later when you are not present.
- Never apologize for your first draft. Do the best you can in your rough draft **and** your personally revised draft, and then turn the essay over to your peer.
- Throw your ego out the window. Peer reviewers are helping you improve your writing and your grade; if they were not available and the essay went directly to the instructor for grading, your grade would probably be lower.
- Focus on global concerns **only**—save any comments on grammar, mechanics, spelling, and formatting for the editing review or workshop.
- Pick and choose what you want to use from your peer reviewer's comments. You might not want to change everything mentioned; however, be sure to consider everything your peer reviewer suggests. Sometimes, others can see what we can't see ourselves, and they can help us get out of an ineffective writing rut.

When Should You Stop Revising?

Most good writing is revised often, so taking time and making a substantial effort is important if you want to improve your writing and your writing grades. Most competent writers can become excellent writers if they have the time to revise their writing significantly before turning it in for evaluation. Multiple drafts are important, and doing significant revision that is separate from significant editing improves all writing.

Although an essay is never really finished, it may be ready to edit when:

- It follows all instructions in the writing assignment.
- It says what you want it to say in the most effective way.
- It sounds right when you or a peer reviewer read it aloud.
- It looks right on the page.
- It has content and a central theme that are fully developed.
- It is well organized.
- It has effective word choices.

How Do You Revise in a Timed Writing Situation?

In-class writing sometimes does not allow time for massive revision; however, you can and should build time into any writing assignment for revision. If given an in-class essay, break the time allowed into short blocks that mimic the parts of the process for an out-of-class essay. If you have 60 minutes, use 5-10 minutes to brainstorm and outline, 30-40 minutes to write the first draft, 5-10 minutes to revise for global concerns, and 5-10 minutes to edit for local concerns. If you are writing on a computer, print out a copy of the paper, if possible, to revise and edit offline. Then, add changes, correct spelling and typos, and print your final draft. Even in a tight writing situation, it pays to always make time for revision and editing.

REVISION GUIDE

(make copies of this page when needed)

Writer:________________________ **Reader:** ______________________

Essay title:____

Directions to the readers: This handout is for general use; follow the specific directions your instructor gives you for this workshop, which is intended to help with revision of content, organization, and word choice only. Answer the following questions about the essay you are reviewing. DO NOT answer the questions with just "yes" or "no"; explain your answers fully, so the writer will have a chance to use your insights to help improve his or her paper. DO NOT edit the paper; this will come in the next workshop.

1. Is there a **title**? Is it interesting? If you answered "no" to either of these questions, suggest a title to the student after you read the entire essay.

2. Does the introductory material work well as an **attention-getter** for you as a reader?

3. How well does the writer keep his or her **audience** in mind?

4. What does the writer's **purpose** seem to be? How could it be clarified?

5. Read the beginning of the essay, and then pause. What is the main idea of the entire essay? **Underline the thesis.** Is the thesis well written and clear? Provide information on how to make either of these things better/more effective.

6. Read only the topic sentences of the body paragraphs in order. Do they give a general outline of the following paragraphs on their own? Does each paragraph have a **topic sentence** that relates directly to the thesis or main point?

7. Look at each of the **body paragraphs** individually now. Does each paragraph have enough support/specific detail? Does each paragraph support the topic sentence given at the beginning of the paragraph?

8. Does the writer use **transitions** to go from one idea to another (between body paragraphs and within body paragraphs)?

9. Should the writer expand on any points? Go to the essay and mark **three** places with an **X** where you think the writer needs to provide more developed and effective details to support the main idea. Next to these, offer suggestions to help the writer revise for more effective support.

10. Look at the **word** level now. Are there word choice problems?

11. What do you like **best** about the entire essay?

PEER REVISION WORKSHEET

(make copies of this page when needed)

Paper's Title:____

Author:____

Reviewer:____

Read the essay several times, and then answer as fully and as helpfully as possible each of the following questions.

1. What is the writer's thesis in the paper? Write a thesis statement, or quote an explicit thesis statement from the paper.

2. Did you like the paper's title? Did it catch your interest? Did it adequately represent the paper's contents?

3. How would you rate the introduction to the paper? Circle one.

   GREAT GOOD ADEQUATE NEEDS WORK

   Now explain why you rated the introduction as you did:

4. How is the body of the paper organized? Do a very brief outline in the space below.

   Does that outline suggest any problem areas? Where? (Circle the area on the outline you just did.)

5. Does the paper have a conclusion, or does it just stop? How would you rate the conclusion? Circle one.

   GREAT GOOD ADEQUATE NEEDS WORK

   Now explain why you rated the conclusion as you did:

6. Make two (2) specific recommendations to the writer.

CHAPTER 5

Editing

What Is Editing?

Editing is the final step of the writing process. As you learned in the last chapter, many students make the mistake of focusing on error correction and proofreading **before** taking the time to develop, clarify, and organize ideas fully through drafting and revision. Although the parts of the writing process are not finite and sometimes do overlap, editing is a separate activity designed to address what writing specialists call **local issues**, such as

- Grammar
- Sentence variety
- Mechanics
- Spelling
- Formatting

When Should You Edit?

Editing should come **after** you feel confident about the choices you have made in content, organization, and style. You might compare editing and proofreading to washing, waxing, and polishing your car—it would be absurd to take the time to do these things to a vehicle that does not run! Drafting and revising ensures that your writing is first fine-tuned; **then,** you edit to make it shine on the surface.

What Are the Different Levels of Editing?

- Paragraphs
- Sentences
- Words
- Proofreading
    - Punctuation
    - Spelling
    - Capitalization and italics
    - Formatting (this can also be considered the essay level)

Paragraph-Level Editing

The first step in editing is to check your paragraphing. Think of paragraphs as larger forms of punctuation that broaden the connections shown by traditional punctuation marks, such as commas, semi-colons, and periods. Punctuation marks indicate pauses, relationships, and connections within and between sentences. Likewise, paragraph indentations and lengths provide readers with visual guidance to relationships and connections between major ideas.

When you begin editing at the paragraph level, ask yourself

1. What does each paragraph **say** (main idea) and **do** (introduce, provide proof or support, give an example, illustrate, connect, conclude)?
   - Begin a new paragraph for each new idea.
   - The order of the paragraphs should be logical.
   - Look at what the paragraphs do, and question the usefulness of each.
2. Are sentences within paragraphs unified and consistent? Check for
   - Unrelated ideas.
   - Illogical sequences and series.
   - Mixed metaphors and/or confusing comparisons.
   - Mismatched subjects and verbs, e.g., *butter reads* or *books believe.*
   - Transitional words or phrases.

Sentence-Level Editing

When you begin editing on the sentence level, ask yourself

1. Are the connections between ideas effectively communicated through subordination and coordination? Check for
   - Short, choppy sentences.
   - Excessively long, hard-to-follow sentences.
   - Unclear emphasis due to faulty or excessive subordination.
2. Are individual sentence structures clear and easy to follow? Check for
   - Misplaced parts.
   - Modifiers that have no referent in the sentence.
   - Modifiers that are too far from the words they modify.
3. Are ideas balanced through the use of parallel elements?
4. Are there any sudden shifts in grammatical structures, tone, or style? Check for
   - Consistent use of verb tense.
   - Consistency in person and number.
   - A unified tone/style.
5. Do sentences vary in length and construction?
6. Are sentences concise, free of deadweight or unnecessary words? Check for
   - Placeholders like *there, it, this,* and *these.*
   - Excessive use of forms of the verb to be—replace with strong, specific verbs.
7. Are sentences direct? Check for
   - Use of active voice—where the subject performs the action of the sentence, e.g., *The registrar misplaced your transcripts.*
   - Purposeful use of passive voice—to avoid assigning blame or for emphasis, e.g., *Your transcripts were misplaced.*
8. Are there any fragments, comma splices, or fused sentences?
9. Do all subjects and verbs agree? Do all pronouns agree with their antecedents? Are all verb forms correct?

Word-Level Editing

When you edit for word choice, ask yourself

1. Are any words vague? Check for
   - General nouns—replace with specific or concrete nouns, e.g., replace *school* with *TAMU-CC* or *vehicle* with *Jeep Wrangler.*

- General verbs—replace with specific, active verbs, e.g., replace *says* with *argues* or replace *ran* with *sprinted.*
- Have you avoided sweeping generalizations that cannot possibly be supported? If not, replace with statements that acknowledge exceptions or qualifications.

2. Are any words or phrases overused? Check for
   - Repeated words at beginnings of sentences.
   - Use of clichés.
3. Have unnecessary words been cut out?
4. Does the vocabulary reflect sensitivity to audience, purpose, and context? Check for
   - Stereotypes.
   - Biased language—based on gender, race, ethnicity, sexuality, religious affiliations, age, or social class.
   - Connotations associated with words—when using a thesaurus, make sure you understand how the word is used and the nuances of meaning associated with the word in various contexts or cultures.
   - Jargon—technical words should be defined or explained.
5. Does your tone (attitude towards the subject) engage your readers? Check for
   - A hostile tone.
   - Assumptions about the readers or their beliefs.
   - The use of *you.*

Proofreading

Punctuation

When you edit for punctuation, ask yourself

1. Do sentences have the correct closing punctuation?
2. Are commas, semi-colons, dashes, apostrophes, and other internal punctuation marks used correctly?
3. Are quotations correctly introduced, punctuated, and carefully cited? Are quotation marks turned the right way—towards the quoted material?
4. Are in-text citations correctly punctuated?

Spelling

When you edit for spelling, ask yourself

1. Are all words spelled correctly? Remember that spellcheckers are **not** always foolproof! Check for commonly confused words.
2. Have you used the correct forms? Double-check any abbreviations, contractions, or possessive nouns.
3. Have you used hyphens correctly? Double-check any hyphenated adjectives.

Capitalization and Italics

When you edit for capitalization and italics, ask yourself

1. Are words capitalized appropriately?
2. Are quotations capitalized correctly?
3. Are proper names and titles distinguished with appropriate capitalization and punctuation?
4. Are titles punctuated correctly with italics or quotation marks?

Formatting

Formatting correctly shows that you care about the presentation of all your hard work. However, looks can be deceiving; a paper that looks good can still contain serious errors. Computers have made it much easier to produce a professional-looking document, but editing is still essential.

When you edit for formatting, ask yourself

1. Have you followed all of your instructor's directions about formatting?
2. Are the margins correct?
3. Is the spacing correct between words, sentences, and paragraphs?
4. Is the assignment block present and correct? Does it contain all of the required information in the correct order and form?
5. Do you have a title that is centered and spaced correctly—and not underlined, italicized, bolded, in quotation marks, or in a different font?
6. Do you have a header with your name and page numbers?
7. If needed, do you have a Works Cited that follows MLA guidelines?

WHAT ARE TEN EFFECTIVE EDITING STRATEGIES?

- Set the work aside for a time after revising.
- Participate in editing workshops if available in your classes.
- Use your resources: previous papers, the Writing Center, and your instructor.
- Know your enemies or problem areas.
- Read aloud, to yourself or to another person, to avoid self-correcting.
- Read backwards to ensure a focus on editing, not revision.
- Learn tricks, such as acronyms like FANBOYS and THINTICs, to help you remember rules or common lists.
- Use your tools. Keep your dictionary, thesaurus, a grammar handbook, class notes and handouts, and Writing Center handouts nearby when editing.
- Have someone else read your work for proofreading errors, clarity, and sensitivity to audience.
- Know that you will **always** have to edit your writing or work. You cannot depend on others to do it for you.

PEER EDITING WORKSHEET

(make copies of this page when needed)

Today we are focusing on editing, not revising. Therefore, I want the author and the peer editor to pay attention to the issues listed below.

Paragraphs

1. On a separate sheet of paper, write a sentence summarizing what each paragraph says and does.

2. Mark any places within paragraphs where sentences lack unity and consistency.

Sentences

1. Mark any places where sentences are unclear, incorrectly constructed, or indirect.

2. Note any unnecessary repetition in sentence lengths and structures.

3. Underline any agreement errors or illogical shifts—subjects-verbs, pronouns-antecedents, verb tense, or point of view.

Words

1. Circle or bold any words that are unclear, vague, or unnecessary. Suggest two replacements for each.

2. Mark any places where words and tone do not reflect sensitivity to audience, context, or purpose. Explain these responses to the writer.

3. Circle or bold any words that are repetitive, overused, or clichéd. Suggest a replacement for each.

Proofreading

1. Place square brackets around any missing or misused commas, semi-colons, colons, dashes, apostrophes, quotations marks, or end punctuation marks.

2. Underline any misspelled words or incorrect/confused forms.

3. Place square brackets around any missing or misused capitalization and/or italics.

4. Note any places in the paper where the formatting fails to follow the instructor's directions.

GRAMMAR GRID

This grid charts the occurrence of the Seven Major Grammar Errors that instructors look for in student papers. The purpose of this grid is to give you a visual representation of your grammar mistakes so that you can chart your progress during the semester. **Remember to closely examine your graded essays when they are returned to you in order to become familiar with your own common errors as a writer.** Keep track of your errors on this worksheet by putting the number of times each error occurs in the appropriate box.

ERROR	Essay #1	Essay #2	Essay #3	Essay #4	Essay #5
Sentence Fragment					
Comma Splice/ Fused Sentence					
Subject/Verb Agreement Error					
Pronoun/Antecedent Agreement Error					
Wrong Form or Tense of Verb					
Missing/Misplaced Possessive Apostrophe					
Misspelled or Confused Word Forms					

CHAPTER 6

Rhetoric

The Elements of Rhetoric

From the time of the ancient Greeks and Romans to our present day, someone has always attempted to alter the lives of others through words; witness the eloquent phrases in the Declaration of Independence, Lincoln's "Gettysburg Address," "Martin Luther King's "I Have a Dream" speech, John F. Kennedy's inaugural address, even the demagoguery of Adolph Hitler and Saddam Hussein. The major power of their words is the power of rhetoric, the art or discipline of writing effectively and persuasively, used to inform or motivate an audience. While Aristotle defined rhetoric as discovering the best means of persuasion in any given situation, this definition might include not only the argumentative but the expository or informative mode of discourse as well. In fact, rhetoric operates in almost every form of writing we find. For this reason, rhetoric is still an important concern of each of us today, primarily because none of us can escape it—not the lawyer, the teacher, the politician, the computer analyst, or the student. We all indulge in and are exposed to rhetoric daily. Therefore, the goal of the class in which you are enrolled and the goal of this text are to raise your awareness of the rhetorical components all around you so you might be more effective in expressing your own ideas as well as more alert to others' use and misuse of rhetoric. This text, through its instructions and exercises, can serve as a guide for you in your move toward communicating your thoughts and feelings through words.

Your tasks as a writer can range from giving the directions for planting a garden to persuading an audience that capital punishment should or should not be abolished. Whether you choose to use the expository or persuasive method, you should understand and be able to use certain rhetorical elements in order to make your ideas more convincing or persuasive. These elements include the writer's purpose, audience, voice, and the situation. While all four elements play a role in every

RHETORICAL ELEMENTS

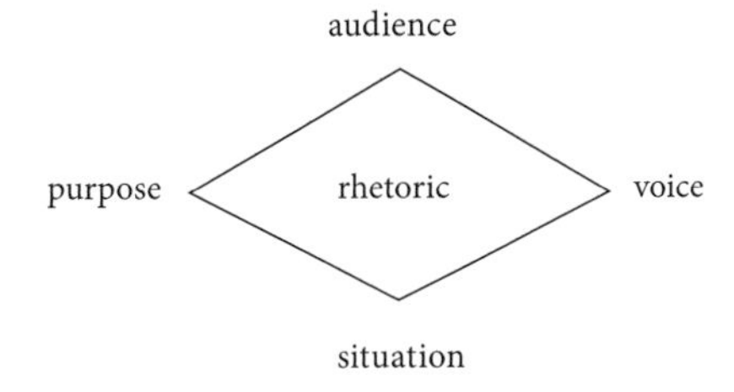

composition, they do not always have equal roles. For example, audience would obviously assume a greater place in process analysis and persuasive essays than in a comparison and contrast essay, and voice might play a minimal role in definition and a major role in narration and description. Nevertheless, each principle must be present for you to achieve your goal of communicating your ideas. However varying their presence in an essay, all four elements must be included.

Purpose

Writing always has a purpose. Every writer must have a reason for writing, and that reason, or purpose, determines which of the other three elements of rhetoric will be emphasized. The general purpose of various writing methods is to know what we think and how best to communicate those thoughts. Therefore, we must always determine what particular message we want to convey and what method would likely be most effective. Do we wish simply to report or inform, to explain, or to persuade? During your college career and afterwards, you might be required to report on a given project or to inform your audience as to the progress of a particular project. In addition, you might be expected to explain to a co-worker the step-by-step procedure for seeking advancement in the company, or you may wish to persuade your supervisor that your particular ideas warrant attention over the proposals of a co-worker. Whichever rhetorical mode you select to write your essay, it must have a purpose, and the purpose must be clearly evident to the reader. The rhetorical purpose is sometimes determined by the specific assignment. If a topic is assigned, your task of deciding on a purpose may already have been done for you. However, often you will have to determine the purpose yourself. If it cannot be discovered immediately, the purpose can emerge from your preliminary brainstorming of the assigned general topic and from the early stages of organizing your random thoughts. Until a purpose is clearly in your mind, though, it is best not to begin writing the essay, else you will likely waste time and effort. Time spent in determining your purpose is far better used than time spent in wandering from point to point without direction. Knowing your purpose helps you sharpen your focus. Make certain, too, that your goals are reasonable and that you can manage what you tell your audience you will accomplish in your statement of purpose, or your thesis. Then you can decide which method of presentation is the most efficient and can best accomplish your purpose.

Audience

Your audience is your intended listener or reader. Every word we utter is directed toward something or someone, even if we are only talking to ourselves. When we speak to someone, we have the advantage of immediate feedback, of noting the reaction, either verbal or nonverbal, and so we are able to determine whether or not he understands us. When speaking, therefore, we can adjust our voice, gestures, or language to accommodate our listener, thus increasing our chances of being understood. In writing, however, the advantages of instant feedback and subsequent adjustments are not available to us. Therefore we must be more aware of who our audience is and what he or she knows. If we want to achieve an intended effect (purpose), we must be able to make certain assumptions about our audience. In adapting your ideas to meet your particular audience, you must bear in mind the interests and values of those you want to reach. Estimate what their backgrounds are, their education, age, sex, political and religious inclinations, and experiences. What can they expect to gain by reading your ideas? These concerns help you establish which approach to use in presenting your ideas and what to stress or to omit in your essay. Identifying the audience will assist you in anticipating questions and in being prepared to address those questions in your essays. This procedure is not unlike a job applicant's research into a company with whom he intends to interview.

Students are correct in assuming their audience is their instructor. But most writing instructors will want you to specify a variety of audiences, real or imagined, in order to sharpen your rhetorical skills to meet the demands of different situations. This task is not always easy. Addressing a variety of audiences in a variety of essays places restraints on students, but these situations more than likely reflect the situations you may encounter in life. You will always be confronted with different audiences, different situations, and different subjects. It is best, then, to keep in mind that you will likely have more than one audience for your essay—your instructor and some other designated audience. This dual audience requires you to adapt to each one's needs and expectations, just as a newspaper reporter must write a news item with his editor as well as the general reading public in mind. Knowing your audience and writing to them does not mean you have to sacrifice your own beliefs in order to accommodate those of your audience. You must not feel you have to choose between your integrity and reader appeal. If you are skillful in the use of rhetoric, you can maintain an honest and authentic voice and at the same time still be a successful strategist.

Voice

Having defined your audience, you must now determine the role that you want to assume with your audience. This stance, or voice, that you must assume is much like the different masks you prepare daily. You present yourself one way when attending class, and you present yourself quite differently when you are on a date or visiting your in-laws. While these masks are different, your identity is still the same. Each role is sincere, but each allows you the flexibility to select the appropriate demeanor and words for a specific occasion and audience. This role-playing is similar to the role you assume in presenting your ideas in your essay to a given audience. Consider how you would express yourself in a personal letter to a friend as compared to how you would express yourself in a letter of application for scholarship funds. Authenticity and sincerity are imperative. They guide the voice in its attempt to demonstrate you are serious about your subject and respectful of your audience. Be genuine in whatever voice you assume. You can be sympathetic, neutral, angry, or humorous, but most of all be yourself. What you say and how you say it, therefore, are determined by your purpose, audience, and subject matter.

Situation

The fourth element of the rhetorical process is the situation. It is the most important of all four elements because without it you would have no basis for an essay. The remainder of this text is concerned with the steps in putting together your ideas and deciding on the appropriate method of presenting those ideas to a designated audience in a given situation. Which arrangement to use in presenting your essay depends upon the situation, your audience, your voice or the stance you take in offering your ideas, and your purpose. The rules for the art and craft of rhetoric are not written in stone, nor are they "writ in water." A great deal of rhetorical flexibility in regard to these rules is available to writers of compositions, but sometimes the refusal to concern yourself with these rules can have disastrous consequences. In the classroom the results can be an inferior grade, while in the marketplace they can mean unemployment. The rules that are discussed in the following pages represent the methods of writing that are time-proven, that have served people in almost every endeavor—mostly, but not always, for good purposes. We can only hope that you use your rhetorical skills for the general good, never to be abused or misused.

So now we arrive at our starting place; through language and the expression of ideas we begin to understand our world and ourselves.

Rhetorical Analysis of an Essay

You probably have already read, and written, a number of essays this semester, and you have probably had occasion throughout your career in school to read numerous short articles in magazines and newspapers or on your computer. In its broadest sense, the word *essay* can cover everything from a short report to a lengthy, technical article. The motives behind essays are also varied. Essays are written to entertain, to explain, to persuade, to justify one's actions, to beg for support or money, to sell, to condemn some person or action, to report on what has been done in an experiment or accomplished on a job, to encourage patriotism, to inflame one group of people against another, to deceive, to express adoration and love— the possibilities are myriad.

Teachers of rhetoric use the more inclusive term *text* to cover such variety, and they add oral communication to the list. Modern critics engage in analyses of such divergent texts as Fourth-of-July speeches, parking regulations, and recipes. Modern critics also approach their texts from an astonishing variety of perspectives: there are sociological critics, feminist critics, historical critics, psychological critics, Marxist critics, cultural critics, post-modern critics. A text to contemporary critics is anything but a group of words whose meaning is carved in stone, and just as there are common elements of fiction that help us to understand and analyze short stories, so there are, though perhaps less standardized than in fiction, elements common to all prose texts.

Elements of Rhetoric

All written texts—whether they are essays or handwritten notes—contain certain common, rhetorical elements. As you analyze an essay or text, you should examine and identify each of the following:

Audience. When you analyze an essay, always try to identify the intended audience of a particular text. The intended audience of an essay, for example, may be identified by looking at the author's style (his diction and sentence structure), the complexity and type of ideas discussed, the essay's length, its purpose and situation, and the persona adopted by the writer. Where an essay is published, in *Time, Field and Stream,* or *Scientific American,* is also a clue to the educational level and interests of the audience. The intended audience is discovered inductively; for example we might determine that the 5:30 evening news is aimed toward an older, conservative, affluent audience by noting the number of advertisements shown during the half-hour for such things as denture cream, investment opportunities, and luxury automobiles.

Purpose. In analyzing an essay you should always attempt to state the author's purpose. What does the writer want the reader to understand, to feel, to do? Writers want to change their readers' beliefs or attitudes, make them laugh, make them cry, make them understand a complex issue. A list of purposes would be very long: to entertain, to persuade, to explain, to frighten, to teach, to anger, to placate.

Situation. All discourse is constrained by the situation in which it appears. Situation, loosely defined, is the context in which a particular text appears or the occasion on which a discourse is delivered. For example, the following are different situations with different contexts: you are required to write a ten-page report on the causes of the Civil War in an American history class; you volunteer to speak to your younger brother's scout troop on tae kwon do; you write a letter applying for a summer job at Yellowstone National park. Each situation or context demands a different response. In analyzing an essay, you should try to determine the situation or context in which the essay was written and the specific constraints such a situation places on what the writer says. Keys to context or situation for published essays include when it was published, in what magazine or journal it is published, and the tone and language employed by the writer.

Voice. The writer reveals his personality, his attitudes, his prejudices and desires through what he says and the way he says it. Just as there is a narrator who tells a story from a particular point of view, just as there is a "voice" in poetry, so there is a speaker in an essay, a persona (in Latin, literally "actor's mask"). A writer may unconsciously reveal the kind of person he is through what he writes. We may determine that he is arrogant, friendly, narrow-minded or flippant. More often the writer's purpose, his audience, and the writing situation cause him to assume or adopt a **persona.** Aristotle says, for example, that when trying to persuade an audience we should present ourselves as honest, open-minded, and knowledgeable, with the best interests of our audience in mind. The persona a writer adopts may also reflect his social or cultural role. For example, we expect a priest and a movie critic to write in certain ways reflecting their different roles and positions in society.

Tone, finally, is closely connected to persona. Writers may adopt tones that are serious, playful, ironic, antagonistic, or passionate, among others. In writing a critical analysis of an essay, you should determine the persona and tone of the writer. Whether consciously or unconsciously revealed, persona is crucial to the total effect a text has on its audience.

Rational Appeals

Aristotle believed that what separated mankind from other animals was the ability to reason. Many writers thus employ rational appeals in an attempt to convince their audiences to accept or reject particular beliefs, claims, or courses of action. When a scientist writes a paper claiming to have discovered a new sub-atomic particle, when a biotechnology lab claims to have discovered the gene that causes Huntington's disease, when an engineer claims that a system of mass-transit will solve a city's transportation problems—all support their claims with evidence and logic. If a writer provides little or no proof for the claims he or she makes, you should be wary of accepting those claims, even though the claims might seem to be true. In addition you should consider the following:

Burden of Proof. A basic principle of reason, as of law, is that the burden of proof rests with the person making a claim. A claim is a proposition, a statement about what is or is not true. If the state claims that Joe Smith murdered his wife, for instance, then the state must prove beyond a reasonable doubt that Joe is guilty; Joe does not have to prove that he did *not* murder his wife. Careful writers will not make claims that they cannot back up. Thus, when you read essays, always look to see what **evidence and support** the writer provides to back up his claims. Further, be wary of non-testable claims. A non-testable claim is set up in such a way that no possible evidence or change in circumstances could render it false. As Stephen Jay Gould writes in *Evolution as Fact and Theory:* "A set of ideas that cannot, in principle, be falsified is not science. . . . Unbeatable systems are dogma. . . ." For example, if someone argues that people *always* act from selfish motives, and no counter example you come up with, no action or set of circumstances you devise, is ever accepted as an example of an unselfish action, it is a non-testable claim; that is, it is an assertion of belief. Beliefs are strongly held attitudes involving judgments about the world and are often accepted as articles of faith, beyond the realm of rational inquiry.

Fallacies. Logicians have identified a number of common fallacies (faulty reasoning that may appear to be good); you need to look for them when you analyze a writer's argument. Refer to p. 59–60 for a list of the most common fallacies.

Toulmin Analysis. In an *Introduction to Reasoning* (1984), Steven Toulmin presents a simple, practical method of reasoning. He divides his argument into an attractive scheme of three primary parts—claim, data (ground), and warrant. There are several categories of claims on which to base one's argument.

Different Types of Claims

A factual claim is a declarative sentence that asserts something is or is not the case, was or was not the case, or will or will not be the case. "Austin is the capital of Texas" is a claim about reality. "Dallas is the largest city in Texas" is a claim about reality. "The Houston Astros will win the pennant" is a claim about the future (We must wait until October for verification of it!) "Socrates lived in ancient Athens" is a claim about the past which can be verified by reading accounts of his contemporaries.

Thus, claims of fact can be **verified** or **falisified.** That is, a factual claim is **true** if it corresponds to reality—or is a **tautology** (something true by definition, such as "A bachelor is an unmarried man.").

A value claim is a declarative sentence that asserts something is good or bad, right or wrong. Some value claims are merely **expressions of personal taste,** of liking or disliking: "Broccoli tasts bad." "I prefer living in the city to living in the country." "I feel hot." Such claims cannot be disputed.

Other value claims are **moral** or **aesthetic judgments:** "Stealing is wrong." "A liberal education is better than a technical one." "Andrew Wyeth is a better painter than Jackson Pollock." Such value claims are supported by reference to a code of morality, an accepted ideal, or a set of criteria the arguer uses as the basis of his claim. The Christian Bible might be the basis for the first claim, the Humanist ideal for the second, and standards of realist painting for the third.

A **causal claim** is a declarative sentence that asserts something is, or was, the cause of something else. "Smoking is a major cause of cancer" is a causal claim. "Slavery was a major cause of the Civil War" is another.

A **definitional claim** is a declarative sentence that asserts something is just like, or is exactly the same as, something else. "Keeping animals in cages is just like keeping slaves in shackles" is such a claim. "Abortion is murder" is another.

A **deliberative claim** is a declarative sentence that asserts that something should or should not be done. These are sometimes called **claims of policy.** "You should quit smoking" is a deliberative claim. "The state of Texas should adopt a law making English its official language" is another deliberative claim.

Following this system, the student would first find the **claim,** the conclusion of the argument or the thesis of the essay. Make sure that the claim is a testable-claim (that it is possible to support the claim by evidence), and that it is not preposterous or whimsical. For example, the following claim was made by a student at North Harris College: "*Women should not be allowed in ground combat units in the army.*"

Next look for the **Grounds** that support that claim, that is, the evidence the writer gives in support of his proposition. For example, the student supported the above claim with the following evidence: "*The fact that a woman can get pregnant may keep her from performing her task, thus rendering the squad ineffective to perform in a combat situation. An example of this situation occurred when I was stationed at Ft. Rucker, Alabama; in my squad there were four men and each of us was assigned a different task: machine gunner, sniper, squad leader, and Dragon gunner. We went on an exercise and the machine gunner became ill. He was rushed to the hospital, and I had to take over his task. The result of his illness was a catastrophe. When we attacked the enemy we were slower because I had to perform the jobs of two men. Therefore, the squad lost the battle, which not only had an effect on the squad but produced a chain reaction and destroyed the whole company. Thus if a woman were to be assigned to a combat unit and she became pregnant, it would have a negative influence on the whole company.*"

Third look for any **Warrant** that the writer gives to show that the evidence is relevant to the claim. For example, if the writer cites the statement of an authority, does he or she give the credentials of the authority? Is the authority speaking in his own field of expertise? If a major scientific study is discussed as evidence, are other confirming studies also cited? For example, the student writing on women in combat added the following to the evidence given above:

> *"More than 1,200 pregnant women were evacuated from the Gulf region during the Gulf War; that is the equivalent of two infantry battalions. If the loss of one man from a squad can cause a company's performance to drop, how much more harm would there be with the loss of two battalions of soldiers? It would have a devastating effect."*

Fourth look for **Backing,** information that gives added support to the Warrant. For example, our student next added the following sentence to the above warrant: *"The statistics on the number of women evacuated from the Gulf War were released in a report by the Pentagon."*

Finally, check to see if the writer has given a **Rebuttal** to counter claims and arguments; that is, has he mentioned and then refuted claims that contradict his own? Also see if the writer has explained apparent exceptions to his evidence or mitigated the force of the counter claim in some way. For example, our student included the following in a refutation section:

> *"Some women argue that many other countries use women in combat roles. This statement is not altogether true. There are very few countries that have women in combat roles. Israel was one of those countries who tried to put women in combat, but they quickly stopped the program because it was a catastrophe. Israel still uses women in its military, but does not allow them in combat."*

Using Toulmin's scheme will help you to see the structure of the argument you are analyzing and the strengths and weaknesses of that argument; however, simply because a writer supplies a warrant and backing for a claim does not mean that his argument is sound or cogent. Be sure to apply the standards of appropriate evidence and reasoning to the argument. Finally, remember that arguments are made to be convincing and that we are daily inundated by the mass media with hundreds of claims. The only rational stance to adopt in a world such as ours is one based on a respect for truth and an attitude of skepticism. In his essay "Of Cannibals," Montaigne says "We should be on our guard against clinging to vulgar opinions and ... we should judge things by light of reason, and not from common rumor."

Emotional Appeals

If all people were as dispassionate as Mr. Spock or Data on the old *Star Trek* series, then an account of the argument of an essay, of its rational appeal, would be the only analysis we would need to make. Yet while all people may be born with the capacity to reason, reasoning well requires knowledge, training, and practice. However, to echo the French eighteenth-century writer Jean Jacques Rousseau, we *felt* before we *thought.* Feeling, Rousseau said, is primary; it, not reason, makes us human. Further, as Antonio R. Damasio, head of neurology at the University of Iowa, has pointed out, "emotions [...] inform the deployment of logic."

Thus, emotions are powerful forces in humans, and while we might think of some people as "lacking feeling," most people are strongly affected by their emotions. In Book II of *The Art of Rhetoric,* on "Emotion," Aristole lists and characterizes eight emotions. They can be classified as positive—calm, friendship, favor and pity, or negative—anger, fear, shame, indignation, envy and jealousy. In his 1872 book, *The Expression of the Emotions in Man and Animals,* Charles Darwin began the modern discussion of the nature and origin of emotions. More recent investigators have emphasized the neurological basis of emotions and have listed eight basic emotions—anger, fear, joy, sadness, acceptance, disgust, surprise and interest or curiosity. Others have divided emotions into "primary" and "secondary" emotions. Robert Plutchik, professor emeritus at the Albert Einstein College of Medicine, lists the eight basic emotions as fear (terror, shock, surprise), anger (rage), sorrow (sadness), joy (happiness, glee), disgust, acceptance, anticipation, and surprise. In an article in *American Scientist* in 2001, he gave a three-dimensional "color wheel" model of the emotions. From "outside-in" the opposed emotions on the wheel are:

> *Pensiveness, Sadness, Grief—Ecstasy, Joy, Serenity Boredom, Disgust, Loathing—Admiration, Trust, Acceptance Distraction, Surprise, Amazement—Vigilance, Anticipation, Interest Annoyance, Anger, Rage—Terror, Fear, Apprehension*

Further, while we consider our emotions *natural,* we know that these emotions are conditioned by our culture, our social background, and our individual upbringing. Writers appeal to their particular audience's emotions in order to motivate them to action or to gain their commitment to a belief or a group. For example, writers are well aware that people respond emotionally to words and images that appeal to certain deep-seated human desires for love, sex, nourishment, and pleasure. Conversely, people respond emotionally to what they fear: rejection, privation, pain, and death. On the one hand, writers appeal to their audience's sense of comfort which they derive from belonging to a group such as a family, city, state, or country, or their affiliation with a certain ethnic or linguistic group, economic class or political party; on the other hand, writers play on their audience's fear and distrust of things or people that are strange or foreign to them.

The language used in emotional appeals can be direct or subtle. Writers can use words that have an obvious and immediate emotional impact on their audience and which are calculated to provoke a strong and predictable response. For instance, how do you react to the following words: *jerk, extremist, atheist, bubba, dumb blonde; or to peace, patriot, Christian, entrepreneur, mother?* For example, note Richard Nixon's use of emotionally charged language in the following paragraph, the conclusion to a famous speech he made on television in September of 1952; at the time many people were calling for his resignation as candidate for vice-president under Dwight Eisenhower because of allegations of misappropriation of campaign funds:

> *But just let me say this last word. Regardless of what happens, I am going to continue this fight. I am going to campaign up and down America until we drive the crooks and the communists and those that defend them out of Washington, and remember, folks, Eisenhower is a great man, and a vote for Eisenhower is a vote for what is good for America.*

The words used in this passage depict two contrasting sets of images. The first set creates the image of a man battling against the forces of evil: "... I am going to continue this *fight* ... until *we* [Note the shift in person. He is one of us.] drive the *crooks* and the *communists* and *those that defend them out of Washington. . . .*" Here is the image of a man trying to drive out evil from one of our political holy places, perhaps like Jesus drove the moneychangers out of the Temple. The second set of words—"*Eisenhower is a great man*" and "what is *good for America*"— evokes the feelings of pride we have in a renowned military leader and associates those feelings with our feelings of patriotism. These feelings of greatness, goodness, and loyalty to our homeland are linked to the lonely fight against evil conducted by this man on our behalf.

The emotion of a passage may also arise naturally from the writer's subject and the intensity of the writer's engagement with that subject. For example, few would question the sincerity of the emotion expressed in the following sentences by the Russian writer Leo Tolstoy who, at the peak of his career as a writer, with fame, wealth, an interesting circle of friends, a family—all that a person could desire—suddenly experienced a terrible, gripping sense of the utter futility of life. He wrote of this life-altering experience in *Confession* (here translated by David Patterson):

> *If not today, then tomorrow sickness and death will come (indeed, they were already approaching) to everyone, to me, and nothing will remain except the stench and the worms. My deeds, whatever they may be, will be forgotten sooner or later, and I myself will be no more. Why, then, do anything? How can anyone fail to see this and live? That's what is amazing! It is possible to live only as long as life intoxicates us; once we are sober we cannot help seeing that it is all a delusion, a stupid delusion! Nor is there anything funny or witty about it; it is only cruel and stupid.*

The intensity of feeling in this passage arises from the writer's emotional involvement with his subjects, death and the meaning of life. Tolstoy conveys his fear of death and his sense of the utter meaninglessness of life in such phrases as "sickness and death will come," "the stench and the worms," and "I myself will be no more." These words are simple, direct, and unadorned. Tolstoy also employs an everyday image of a drunk versus a sober man to convey his feelings about everyman's blindness to the reality of his own death. The emotions we feel when we read such a passage arise directly from the subject and the writer's engagement with it. Tolstoy's primary purpose is to convey his feelings, to make us feel what he himself feels.

In writing a critical analysis of an essay that focuses on its emotional content, therefore, you will need to look carefully for any emotionally charged words used by the writer, at any images the writer creates through description, and at any figurative language the writer uses (see the section on analysis of style later in this chapter). In addition, ask yourself the following questions:

How important is the writer's use of emotion to the overall purpose of the essay?

Is the writer's use of emotion appropriate to the subject and occasion?

Does the writer's use of emotionally charged language dominate the essay, or is it subordinated to more rational arguments?

Is the writer's use of emotion effective and consistent with his purpose?

Answering these questions will also help you decide what the writer's attitude is toward his material and his audience. For example, is the writer asking the reader to sympathize or be outraged? Is the writer being satiric or ironic?

Finally, what can an analysis of the emotional appeals made in an essay tell us? First, it can clarify a complex argument by helping us separate the emotional appeals from the logical ones. Focusing on the language and metaphors employed by the writer in developing his emotional appeal can help us gain emotional distance, and thus objectivity. Therefore we may begin to notice that the writer gives little solid evidence to support his claims and essentially begs the question he is trying to prove. Or we may find that the emotional language drives home a point abundantly supported by evidence and reason. Second, an analysis of the emotional language and appeals in a speech or an essay can sensitize us to the sometimes subtle assault on our emotions made in newspapers and magazines, or over television and radio by politicians, preachers, teachers, and radio talk show hosts (and overwhelmingly in advertisements). Studying the emotional appeals made even in a single essay can help us to understand and to arm ourselves against such assaults. Emotions are very powerful; be wary of allowing yours to be manipulated.

Ethical Appeals

Besides being rational and emotional creatures, humans are also moral beings. We all like to think of ourselves as "being good" and "doing what is right." Thus, if writers can convince us that what they propose for us to do or believe is moral, just, or right, we will more easily go along with them. Such appeals are what Aristotle called *ethical appeals.* In making an ethical appeal, a writer may appeal to our religious beliefs (adultery may be condemned because it is forbidden in the Bible), to our sense of fair play (we may be told that eliminating the capital gains tax will unfairly benefit the very rich who already pay few taxes), to our belief in law (we may be told that we should not smoke marijuana because it is illegal), to our sense of loyalty to an ideal (it may be argued that political action committees should be severely curtailed because they are inherently undemocratic), or to our empathy for fellow humans (all people deserve to have food and shelter).

The power of ethical appeals comes from their assumption of moral authority. If a writer's audience is composed of strong believers in the Bible, for instance, the writer can use scripture as a source of authority. Yet someone who does not accept the moral force of the Bible will hardly be convinced by references to scripture. The same is true of other groups. Some of the most intractable of contemporary conflicts derive from the fact that different groups have different moral bases for their beliefs. Again, to echo Aristotle, in making an ethical appeal writers appeal to what their audience considers to be good or right over and above what they consider useful or in their own interest. For example, Jane Goodall makes an essentially ethical appeal when she states that "all except the most primitive of non-human animals experience pain, and . . . 'higher' animals have emotions similar to the human emotions that we label pleasure or sadness, fear or despair." She implies that, since animals have feelings just as we do, it is no more right for us to subject them to suffering than it would be for us to subject other humans to suffering. Rhetorically, she asks: "How can we, the citizens of civilized, western countries, tolerate laboratories which—from the point of view of animal inmates—are not unlike concentration camps?" Her point is that no matter what benefits we receive, it is simply wrong to experiment on animals.

Another way of making an ethical appeal is for writers to present themselves as knowledgeable, complete, and fair. That is, they present themselves as reasonable and trustworthy. They do this, as you can in your own essays, first by showing that they know a lot about the subject. They may reveal their credentials (their college degrees, their current position in government or at a university for example), they may discuss the research they themselves have done or discuss a wide range of research conducted by others (up-to-date research, of course), or they may provide convincing examples and other support for their generalizations and conclusions. Second, they may show their thoroughness by their consideration of all relevant material and points of view that have a bearing on their subject. Finally, they may show their fairness by considering opposing points of view and differing interpretations of the facts, by discussing those other positions courteously, and by acknowledging the strengths of those positions where reason demands they should.

Writers are like trial lawyers; they must convince their readers. While it is a popular cliché that "facts speak for themselves," we should be mature enough to realize that they don't; they must be given a voice and a context by a speaker or a writer, and that voice shapes the way we understand the facts.

Analysis of Style

Jonathan Swift described style as proper words in proper places. Today the word **style** is used in a number of different ways to describe such things as fashion, written formats (as in letter style), and the way people live (as in lifestyle). Written prose style reflects the education, experience, and habits of thought of the writer as well as the basic elements of rhetoric: purpose, audience, and situation. Style is also part of the argumentative and emotional design of an essay. The clarity and force of an argument depend as much on style as on logic; likewise the emotional impact of an essay depends heavily on style.

To analyze a writer's style you must focus on the words a writer uses and the way those words are arranged in phrases, clauses, sentences, and paragraphs. The purpose of a stylistic analysis is to show how a writer's language, sentence structure, and imagery contribute to his overall purpose and design (or how they contradict it) as well as the way they reveal the writer's attitude toward his subject matter and audience. You can approach a stylistic analysis in one of two ways:

1. You can take one element of style, say the writer's use of figurative language, and analyze the entire essay in terms of this one element alone.
2. You can take a single paragraph, or several related short paragraphs, and do a more complete analysis of several elements of style.

In general, a writer's style depends on the way she uses the following:

Diction. The kinds of words writers choose, their *diction,* depend upon their educational and linguistic background and upon the audience and purpose of their essay. We can arrange words along a scale based upon an analogy with social custom. For example, just as men wear suits and ties on serious and formal social occasions, so writers use formal diction on serious occasions and for serious purposes.

Formal diction is characterized by polysyllabic words, many with Latin and Greek roots *(transference, multidimensional, orthodox),* abstract words *(cognitive, affective, discipline)* and words specific to a particular science or profession (medical terminology or computerese for example). Formal diction contributes to a formal style, which is also characterized by its objectivity and the writer's use of the third person, both of which distance the writer from the reader. Formal diction is often used in college textbooks, scientific journals, and philosophical essays; formal style is standard for exposition of serious subjects directed to educated audiences.

At the other end of the scale, comparable to men wearing T-shirts, cut-off shorts, and tennis shoes, is highly informal diction. Informal diction is characterized by monosyllabic words, many with Anglo-Saxon roots (short, familiar words such as *man, run, fish, speak),* colloquialisms, dialect *("y'all"),* slang, contractions, and non-standard usage *("ain't").* Informal diction more closely copies everyday speech and contributes to an informal style, characterized by its subjectivity and the writer's use of first person, which brings the writer and the audience closer together. Informal diction is used in personal letters, the personal essay, and all sorts of short, written communication. As always, audience and purpose are important in the degree of informality of one's diction and one's style. In between these two poles (say, a man wearing loafers, slacks and an open-necked shirt) is a broad range of diction that incorporates words from both ends to a greater or lesser degree.

Besides the degree of formality or informality of the diction of an essay, you can also look at whether the words a writer chooses tend to be more abstract or more concrete, more general or more specific, or more dependent on denotation or connotation.

Concrete words stand for things that you can touch and see, such as *book, desk, cat,* and *fireplace.* Writers use concrete words to help us visualize what we read. **Abstract words,** such as *honor, justice, love,* and *discourse* do not call up specific images; nevertheless we have some way of visualizing them: we can picture a child in the arms of its mother when we read the word *love,* for example. Even more removed from our ability to visualize, however, are certain super-abstract words generally deplored by most good writers as **jargon;** *factor, case, condition,* and *degree* are examples. It is very hard to visualize a *factor.* Concrete diction contributes to a more familiar style and brings us closer to the writer: we see what the writer has seen; we feel what the writer has felt.

Likewise, **specific words** bring up specific images, while **general words** help us to group classes of things. Again, we can set up a scale with very general words on one end and very specific ones on the other: *creature, animal, human, male, boy, son, Daniel.* Good writers are always moving between the general and the specific, going from one end of the scale to the other as they move between broad statements of ideas and issues and specific, detailed examples. Specific language helps us see how large philosophical, moral, or political issues affect us on a personal level. We want a wide-angle lens to show us the big picture; we need a telephoto lens to show us the details.

Finally, writers use words for their limited, **denotative** meaning or for their emotional associations, their **connotations.** Think of another scale with scientists on one end using words for their specific meanings and poets on the other end using words that have multiple meanings and wide associations. A writer's purpose and audience are again extremely important. A politician at a political rally, for example, may use such evocative words as *freedom, democracy, free enterprise,* and *family.* A scientist at the other extreme may use words like *dorsal, ventral,* and *suture* that have precise meanings. Scientists want to communicate their ideas directly and clearly; they neither want the confusion that might arise from using words that have multiple meanings nor the emotional reactions that highly connotative words might create.

Syntax. Syntax designates the way words are combined to form phrases, clauses, and sentences. One way to analyze a writer's prose style is to look at the sentences she habitually uses. For example, some writers use longer sentences than others, piling up phrases and clauses within a single sentence. Others prefer short, more direct sentences. The sentences of the American authors William Faulkner and Ernest Hemingway provide a classic example of this contrast:

> *The boy, crouched on his nail keg at the back of the crowded room, knew he smelled cheese, and more: from where he sat he could see the ranked shelves close-packed with the solid, squat, dynamic shapes of tin cans whose labels his stomach read, not from the lettering which meant nothing to his mind but from the scarlet devils and the silver curve of fish—this, the cheese which he knew he smelled and the hermetic meat which his intestines believed he smelled coming in intermittent gusts momentary and brief between the other constant one, the smell and sense just a little of fear because mostly of despair and grief, the old fierce pull of blood ("Barn Burning,"* William Faulker*).*

> *The girl stood up and walked to the end of the station. Across, on the other side, were fields of grain and trees along the banks of the Ebro. Far away, beyond the river, were mountains. The shadow of a cloud moved across the field of grain and she saw the river through the trees ("Hills Like White Elephants,"* Ernest Hemingway*).*

The passage from Faulkner shows his preference for complex sentences with clauses embedded within clauses. The sentence is evocative and rich with emotional overtones. The passage from Hemingway, however, shows his preference for short, simple sentences. The prose is direct and disarmingly simple.

What can we learn from an analysis of the sentence structure of such writers? First, we can gain insight into what might be called the "world view" or the psychological perspective of the writer. Faulkner's complex sentences reflect the complex world portrayed in his novels—a world where narrators try to recapture the past in recursive attempts to understand and reinterpret the present. Hemingway's habitual use of short, simple, subject-verb-object sentences reflects his belief, also portrayed in his fiction, that life is lonely and harsh and must be confronted directly with simple dignity. Second, a study of sentence structure can help us understand the power, effectiveness, and emotional impact of writing as well as learn, through an understanding of such techniques as repetition and parallelism, how to replicate such effects in our own sentences.

To determine sentence length, for example, count the number of words in each sentence in several paragraphs and divide by the number of sentences to get an average word length per sentence. (Count all the words, including function words such as articles and prepositions.) You might also count the number of very short sentences, say those under eight words, and the number of very long sentences, say those over thirty words. Again, to determine the frequency of the different types of sentences, count the number of sentences by type in several paragraphs. Determining sentence length and type, for example, tells us how well writers develop their topics, how detailed their explanations are, and how much they qualify their generalizations. Some writers hammer home their points with short, direct blows; others allow us to follow the chain of reasoning that leads them to subtle and complex truths. One benefit of an analysis of this sort is that you can compare the length and type of your author's sentences to your own; you may find that clarity is not necessarily the result of short, simple sentences, nor is brevity always the soul of wit.

Sentences are also defined as being **loose**—where the main clause or idea comes first and qualifying statements and dependent clauses are tacked on, or **periodic**— where the dependent clauses and qualifying statements come first and the main clause comes at the end. For example, consider the following two sentences:

> *I waited three long days in your outer office, continually embarrassed by the number of people who came, waited a short while, and went in, smirked at by secretaries traipsing in and out, and feeling degraded by the position of beggar I had to assume.*
>
> *Continually embarrassed by the number of people who came, waited a short while, and went in, smirked at by secretaries traipsing in and out, and feeling degraded by the position of beggar I had to assume, I waited three long days in your outer office.*

The first sentence trails off after the main clause about waiting for three days in an outer office by simply adding details, one after the other. The reader focuses on each added detail but in the process relegates the earlier ones to the back of the mind. By the end of the sentence, the importance of the three-day wait has waned. In the second sentence, however, tension and suspense are built up as we add one detail to the next because we don't know what they refer to. The answer explodes at the end, and we feel the frustration and sense of indignity the writer has had to endure for three long days. We usually write words one after the other, adding details, descriptions, and explanations as we think of them, following the normal subject-verb-object pattern of English. Loose sentences are thus the workhorses of prose; periodic sentences add drama, suspense, and intensity.

There are other qualities of syntax that are important in analyzing prose style. Books on rhetoric devote much time to such qualities, including the methods writers use to expand and collapse sentences, the way they use particular punctuation marks to achieve certain effects, and their methods of opening and closing sentences. Prominent among these other qualities are the ways writers employ **parallel sentence structure, antithesis,** and **repetition.**

English demands, for example, that parallel or equal grammatical structures be used on either side of a coordinating conjunction: *"cat and dog," "running and playing," "jump and shoot,"* but not *"running and jump."* English also demands parallel grammatical structures in series: *"books, magazines, newspapers and television,"* but not *"books, magazines, and decided to leave."* Writers employ more elaborate schemes of parallelism to develop parallel ideas and to give force to them. Consider the emotional impact of the following two sentences:

But, in a larger sense, we cannot dedicate—we cannot consecrate—we cannot hallow—this ground. (Lincoln's *Gettysburg Address*). In this justly famous sentence, Lincoln emphasizes his inability to say anything that could remotely capture the sacrifice and heroism of the men who fought at Gettysburg. By repeating the same phrase, "we cannot," three times, and by raising the importance and force of the verb each time—going from the rather mundane "dedicate" to the more spiritual "consecrate" and finally to the holy and sanctified "hallow"—Lincoln's sentence does what he says he cannot do.

In such condition, there is no place for industry, because the fruit thereof is uncertain: and consequently no culture of the earth; no navigation, nor use of the commodities that may be imported by sea; no commodious building; no instruments of moving, and removing, such things as require much force; no knowledge of the face of the earth; no account of time; no arts, no letters; no society; and which is worst of all, continual fear, and danger of violent death; and the life of man, solitary, poor, nasty, brutish, and short. (Thomas Hobbes's *Leviathan*). In this sentence, Hobbes describes man in a state of nature, before the advent of civilization. The sentence builds on a series of parallel "no" clauses indicating the bareness and harshness of man's condition without the rules and laws of society. It ends in a climax of short, parallel adjectives that have the force of machine gun bullets.

Sentences employing **antithesis** balance contrasting ideas in parallel structures. We use *but* or *or* instead of and many times to signal a contrasting idea. In the following opening lines (the sentence continues), from *A Tale of Two Cities*, Charles Dickens expresses the glaring contradictions in French society on the eve of the French Revolution: *It was the best of times, it was the worst of times, it was the age of wisdom, it was the age of foolishness, it was the epoch of belief, it was the epoch of incredulity, it was the season of Light, it was the season of Darkness, it was the spring of hope, it was the winter of despair....*

Repetition of words, phrases, and sometimes whole sentences is used to drive home a point or build suspense or tension within a paragraph or essay. A famous example is the speech of Marc Antony in Act III, scene ii of Shakespeare's *Julius Caesar* where Antony repeats the ironic phrase "Brutus is an honourable man" four times in a short speech to the Roman mob. Look at the repetition in the following lines by Martin Luther King:

> *I have a dream that one day on the red hills of Georgia, sons of former slaves and sons of former slave-owners will be able to sit down together at the table of brotherhood.*
>
> *I have a dream that one day, even the state of Mississippi, a state sweltering with the heat of injustice, sweltering with the heat of oppression, will be transformed into an oasis of freedom and justice.*
>
> *I have a dream my four little children will one day live in a nation where they will not be judged by the color of their skin but by the content of their character. I have a dream today!*

The repetition of the phrase "I have a dream" emphasizes the fact that freedom, equality, and justice for African-Americans are still *only* dreams. Yet the repetition also affirms Dr. King's belief in change and the ultimate goodness and brotherhood of all men. The phrase, repeated a number of times in the entire speech, rings in the ear like the repetitions in a prayer.

Figures of Speech. Finally, writers many times use figures of speech to shock or surprise their readers, to emphasize a point, or to clarify their ideas. For example, Jane Goodall uses simile and metaphor when she speaks of laboratories that are "not unlike concentration camps," and says that many chimpanzees "live out their lives as prisoners, in bondage to man."

In analyzing the style of an essay, you should not simply *point out* parallel sentence structures or figures of speech; you should explain how such elements of style contribute to the clarity, purpose, or force of the essay as a whole. For example: Does the writer use specific and concrete diction to help us visualize the ideas? Parallel sentence structure to help us grasp equal points? Repetition to help us keep complicated discussions in order? Further, does the style of the essay fit the purpose and situation of the essay? Does the writer use a formal style for a serious subject or formal occasion, or a formal, perhaps inflated style, for a trivial subject? (Sometimes a contrast between style and subject is a deliberate attempt to create humor or satire.) Finally, do the stylistic features of the essay contribute to or detract from the force or emotional impact of the essay? Is the writer deliberately trying to arouse our emotions with the choice of diction and sentence structure, or simply trying to convey his or her own feelings? Is the writer teaching us or preaching to us? As you can see, style is a complicated, integral part of all writing that directly creates meaning in an essay and not just a flourish added by a writer to make his prose "pretty" or "important."

Writing a Rhetorical Analysis of an Essay

Writing a critical analysis of an essay is not an easy task, but it can be made easier if you follow a plan and avoid some common mistakes. Keep in mind that your general purpose in writing a critical analysis is to explain and evaluate what the author has written.

First, follow a logical plan in preparing and writing your essay:

1. Read the essay to gain a general understanding of its purpose and meaning, underlining and writing notes in the margin to mark important passages.
2. Outline the essay, focusing on the thesis and the major supports of that thesis (evidence, examples, explanations, extended arguments, causes, effects, and so on). If the writer fails to support his or her claims, or if he or she uses colorful, emotional language, be sure to note these facts. Making this outline will give you a much clearer idea of the structure and scope of the essay.
3. Make a decision about what critical approach to take in analyzing your chosen essay. You might want to focus on the writer's use of the rational, emotional, or ethical appeals, or perhaps you might do an analysis of the author's style as it is exhibited in a single paragraph or several related paragraphs.
4. Now that you have chosen an approach, read the essay again, listing or otherwise noting examples of the types of support, instances of sound or cogent (or of fallacious) reasoning, or emotive language you want to emphasize in your essay.
5. Organize the material you have isolated, draw your conclusions, set up a thesis, and write your paper.
6. Be sure to mention the author's full name and the complete title of the essay in your introduction.
7. Finally, be sure you give your essay a precise, descriptive title such as ***"Audience Appeal In 'Letter from Birmingham Jail.'"***

Second, avoid the following mistakes in writing your rhetorical analysis:

1. Be sure that you have a **critical** thesis and not a **descriptive** one. A critical thesis is one that states an *evaluation* or *judgment* of an essay based on your analysis of it. For example: *In "Some Thoughts on the Exploitation of Non-Human Animals," Jane Goodall mounts a strong emotional appeal by using highly connotative language, vivid figures of*

speech, and an effective moral analogy. A descriptive thesis, however, merely summarizes what the author says in the essay: *In "Some thought on the Exploitation of Non-Human Animals," Jane Goodall says that experimenting on animals, even if it benefits humans, is morally wrong.* This thesis will lead the writer merely to summarize what Goodall **says** in her essay; it provides no **analysis** of what she says.

2. Keep in mind that assertions are not arguments but judgments; they must be supported with details and examples drawn from the essay. For example, if you say that Goodall engages in fallacious reasoning, you must name the fallacies she uses and give examples of them drawn from the text. You must also tie in what the author says to the point you are making. Don't say merely that "Goodall uses emotionally charged words, such as 'concentration camps,' 'suffering,' and 'heartless monsters.'" Instead, for example, say that "Goodall's use of words and phrases such as 'concentration camps,' 'suffering,' and 'heartless monsters' helps to develop her emotional appeal by causing the reader to think of scientists as cruel and inhuman."
3. Do not write about your chosen essay in the past tense; use the historical present: "not "Goodall *said* ..." but Goodall *says* ..."

Argumentation

Argument usually suggests to us a negative activity. We tend to think of argument synonymously with a quarrel or disagreement; we argue with parents, spouses, or friends. This use of the term, however, differs from its original and still primary meaning, which is associated with reason and objectivity. It is defined as the process of demonstrating, through reason, the likelihood or necessity of a given proposition. The end of argument is persuasion, achieved through reasoning. It is the process of influencing others to respond as we wish them to respond, to assent to the proposition of the speaker or writer.

If everyone always agreed on everything, there would be no need for argument. But we know that disagreements do exist at all levels of life. The fact that some of our disagreements are ancient ones suggests the difficulty people have in reaching agreement. For example, consider a few of the present day controversial topics— abortion, censorship, capital punishment. These controversies will never approach resolution until the truth is discovered and there is agreement as to that truth. Yet how can truth be discovered until there is a free and open encounter between opposing views? This sincere encounter with our differences is the heart of argumentative discourse; therefore, it must be addressed reasonably, objectively, and thoroughly. Once we feel we have touched upon the truth of an argument, we must then strive for assent by persuading others of the correctness of that truth. This attempt at persuasion is a complicated undertaking. To gain our reader's assent to our propositions, we must organize them in a format that will present our ideas most effectively. Since rhetoric is the art of using language effectively, logically we would want to use a rhetorical format, a long-established method that would assist us in presenting our argument and in persuading the reader. The end of persuasion, after all, is assent to the proposition of the speaker or writer, while the end of argument is truth as determined through reasoning. Strictly speaking, then, logic is a means of persuasion. Although their differences are vast, both argument and persuasion have the same goal: to convince for the purpose of assent. Therefore, we will treat these two forms, argumentation and persuasion, as one in our discussion of argumentation.

IMPLEMENTATION

We are all expected on occasion to explain our ideas. When we engage in such an explanation, we call upon evidence to convince our listener or reader that our ideas are true and correct and, therefore, worthy of attention. Sometimes we are expected to present and defend our ideas in writing. For example, in your academic career and in the workplace you will be called upon to analyze situations and texts and to argue for or against certain ideas or opinions. From small businesses to large corporations, employees who can articulate their views logically have an advantage in being considered for advancement. As a student, a citizen, a parent, an employee, or a consumer, you will have many opportunities to express your ideas. Being familiar with argumentative skills will improve your chances of being convincing and persuasive. In addition, you will be able to use these same skills in distinguishing between truth and falsehood in the world around you. Being familiar with the tools of persuasive discourse, you will be able to determine the correctness of claims made by political figures, employers, salespeople, advertisers, and friends. You can then not only determine the validity of others' arguments, but also formulate your own strategy of reasoned argument to counter the beliefs with which you disagree.

In a composition class, however, you will most likely be asked to present your views on a given controversial issue. Based on the topic assigned to you or the topic you select, you must determine what your purpose is. Do you intend to persuade by offering a defense or an attack? Since you will be expected to argue your views in an attempt to persuade your reader to see the issues as you do and, possibly, to act upon the views or recommendations you have prescribed, you must understand and be able to use effectively the rhetorical elements involved in writing persuasive arguments. In addition, you will be expected to identify your specific audience for your essay. The audience determines the approach you take to your argument. With your purpose and audience in mind, you must take a stand on your topic, present a proposition that reflects your stand, and provide evidence to support that stand.

Audience. You must first have a clear understanding of who your audience will be. Your audience will shape a great deal of what you say and how you say it and will guide you in determining your particular approach to your topic. First, your language must be appropriate for your reader. It would be unwise to address a group of junior high school readers with complex language and reasoning, just as it would be imprudent to address a group of experts on your topic in a manner that assumes no knowledge on their part. You must always be both intelligible to and respectful of your audience. In addition, knowing who your audience is allows you to make certain assumptions about that audience in order to select the appropriate and most convincing points to be discussed and the particular appeals to use in the essay. It also gives you the ability to anticipate what objections your audience will have to your ideas. You must assume that your audience is intelligent, informed about your topic, and not only opposes your position but resists it. By assuming an opposing audience you most likely will be prompted to offer a better argument and counter argument (refutation), making your stand on a given topic stronger and more convincing.

While argument begins in conflict, it should end in some form of resolution. Even if your reader is yet unconvinced that you are right and he is wrong, the most you can realistically expect to achieve in a sound argument is that your reader is willing at least to admit to some credibility of your argument. Remember that the fact that your topic is centered in controversy suggests that both schools of thought believe themselves correct in their thinking. Your opponent will probably have at least one sound argument as well. Keep this fact in mind when you are organizing and presenting your argument: this assumption can work to your advantage.

Definition of Terms. Many arguments fail because the writer does not define the terms on which his essay is based. For your audience to understand your ideas, make certain you clearly define the terms you discuss. State, for example, what you mean by "sexual harassment," "censorship," "pornography," "aesthetic value," or "redeeming quality." You must define any term your audience, for one reason or another, risks misunderstanding. Consult a dictionary or construct your own definition based on your understanding of the term and on the manner in which you discuss the term in your argument.

Methods of Appeal

Because persuasion is an attempt to make your ideas and proposals attractive to an audience, you should be familiar with the methods you might use to appeal to that audience. Aristotle identified these appeals as forms of argument: the emotional (pathos), ethical (ethos), and logical (logos) appeals. These three appeals are interwoven throughout the essay, but you must understand how each works and when to use it. With your audience and purpose clearly in mind, you must determine what effect you wish to achieve in your essay and integrate the appeals accordingly in your argument.

Emotional Appeal

When we want to persuade an audience, we often find it necessary to appeal to the personal nature of our topic. People are generally more interested in those matters that touch their hearts than in statistics or logic. The writer of a persuasive argument cannot ignore the fact that much of our identity resides in our emotions and imaginations. If we are to convince readers, we must appeal to their emotions, attempting to ascertain which of our emotions they will accept or approve. The clever writer can then use certain associations which will elicit the desired emotional response in his audience. For instance, if you are addressing a religious group, you might associate the idea of human leadership or fellowship with Christ. This reference links the writer's own propositions to what the audience already identifies with and respects. Sometimes a well-placed word or phrase will enhance the emotional appeal of an argument, as when a writer of an essay against pornography mentions "innocent" children. Conversely, you must remember that this same knowledge of the emotional character of your audience suggests what not to use in your appeal. It would be unwise to think that you could evoke a sympathetic response from a group of Ku Klux Klan members, for instance, while soliciting support for the civil rights movement.

The emotional appeal should never be used exclusively, however. Many feel that appealing to people's emotions is suspect because it can be considered an attempt to manipulate them. Using emotions to manipulate others cannot be condoned in any fashion, but when emotions are used appropriately and in accord with your audience, they can be a very powerful and persuasive element of argumentation.

Ethical Appeal

The ethical argument or appeal is, according to Aristotle, the most potent of all the means of persuasion. For writers' arguments to be effective, their ethos must be apparent in their work and realized by their readers. Simply because a writer presents an argument does not mean that he or she can expect the reader's assent, or even attention; nor can the mere presence of sincerity or emotion bring about the desired assent. To determine the nature of the ethical appeal, one must understand that the writer's words have emotional associations as well as definite meanings. Although the ethical appeal is not restricted by any given specific rules or qualities, certain components can be discussed. For example, three major qualities of the ethical appeal illustrate how the writer can reveal his or her character through the words the writer chooses.

These three components that the writer must make apparent to the reader might be called **good sense, good will,** and **good moral character. Good sense** suggests that the writer is capable of making practical decisions and choosing the proper means to achieve an end. It must be apparent to the reader that the writer is confident in his argument and that it is, in fact, correct and that he views his topic in the proper perspective. **Good will,** the second component, consists in the writer's making clear to his audience that he has nothing but good will towards them. He must demonstrate that he shares their good intentions and basic aspirations and that he shares, too, some of their biases and prejudices, if necessary. The third component, **good moral character** is successfully presented if the writer convinces his audience that he would not deceive them. To acquire this trust, the writer must be sincere and believable. He must show that he knows right from wrong. His attitude and presentation must convince the reader that he is fair and trustworthy.

Keep in mind that the ethical appeal emerges throughout the essay. It is not something a writer merely inserts between paragraphs or ideas. A writer's ethos develops as he or she makes clear to the reader the possession of all three of the components: the heart is genuine, the intentions good, and the recommendations worthy of the reader's attention.

Rational Appeal

The rational appeal is used to convince an audience that the writer's claims are true. To construct an argument using the rational appeal, the writer employs **induction** and **deduction,** both forms of logic. But in order to employ the rational appeal effectively, the writer must first understand some basic concepts and terms of logic:

Logic

A method of distinguishing between correct and incorrect reasoning. Since reasoning is represented in arguments, logic is a method for evaluating arguments.

Argument

An organized discussion of an idea or an issue. It can proceed from a premise or several premises to a conclusion, or it can start with a claim and then give evidence to support that claim. An argument is meant to persuade its readers or listeners that the belief or position held by the arguer is true.

Proposition

A statement that affirms or denies the truth of something. It can be as concrete and as easily verified as the statement *Houston is the largest city in Texas,* or as abstract and difficult to prove as the statement *The soul is immortal.*

Arguments are composed of two types of propositions or claims.

Premises. The propositions stated by the arguer as evidence for the belief that he or she is trying to prove. If possible, the arguer should select premises that will be readily accepted by the audience. Otherwise it will be necessary for the arguer to devise side arguments to show that the premises of the main argument are true.

Conclusion. The proposition expressing the belief that the arguer is trying to persuade the hearer or reader to accept. In a good argument the conclusion follows logically from the premises.

A sound or cogent argument not only provides evidence that its claims are **true,** it also makes sure that its conclusions are **validly** drawn from its premises.

Truth

The situation in which a proposition corresponds to reality or expresses a tautology (truth by definition). Correspondence with reality can only be determined empirically, that is through observation and experience. For example, the statement that the sun is approximately 93,000,000 miles from earth can be verified by experiment. Truth by definition is a matter of how speakers of a language have agreed (often implicitly) upon meanings of words. For example, the statement that bachelors are unmarried men is true because "unmarried men" and "bachelors" mean the same thing in English.

Validity

The process by which arguments are determined to be correct. An argument is valid if its conclusion is properly drawn from its premises: if the rules of logic have been followed in proceeding from premise to conclusion.

Deductive Reasoning

Deduction is a strict form of argument aiming for the strongest possible connection between premises and conclusion. The writer using deductive reasoning aims to set forth evidence so that if the premises are true, the conclusion necessarily follows as true. Alternatively, the writer tries to make it impossible for the premises to be true and the conclusion false. For example, if

A = B

C = A

Necessarily C = B is true

The above example is a *syllogism,* which is a form of deductive argument. There are several types of syllogisms, but the one most commonly known and used is the **categorical syllogism.** The categorical syllogism is composed of two premises and a conclusion, as in the following example:

Parts

Major Premise All men are mortal.

Minor Premise Socrates is a man.
Conclusion Socrates is mortal.

Terms

Major term The predicate of the conclusion (mortal)

Minor term The subject of the conclusion (Socrates)

Middle term The term common to both premises but not included in the conclusion (man/men)

Checklist for Categorical Syllogisms

1. The middle term must be distributed at least once. That is, we must say something about all or no members of the class to which the middle term belongs.
2. There must be only three terms.
3. If a term is distributed in the conclusion, it must be distributed in the premises.
4. If both premises are affirmative, the conclusion must be affirmative.
5. If one premise is negative, the conclusion must be negative.
6. If both premises are negative, no valid conclusion is possible.

Enthymemes

An enthymeme is a syllogism with one of its premises omitted. In order to test the validity of the syllogistic argument, we must supply the omitted premise.

Example 1. He couldn't have stolen that money; he is a church deacon.

Suppressed premise: Church deacons do not steal.

Example 2. They must be rich because they spend every summer in Europe.

Suppressed premise: People who spend their summers in Europe are rich.

Example 3. You can't deny a criminal his natural rights; after all, he is a human being.

Suppressed premise: Humans cannot be denied their natural rights.

A danger in using an enthymeme is that your readers may not recognize it as an enthymeme and, therefore, fail to realize the full import of your argument. The advantage, however, is that if the enthymeme is recognized it creates greater reader involvement in the argument and the essay as a whole.

While your thesis can be a statement that contains the whole syllogism, it can be shortened to include only an enthymeme. If you choose to use the enthymeme as your thesis, as in the examples above, you must still discuss the omitted premise in the body of the essay. Sometimes you may not want to use the syllogism or enthymeme as your thesis. Even though you employ deductive argument and it is based on a syllogism, you may have a thesis statement independent of the syllogism. For example, suppose that your discussion is organized around a syllogism that shows the validity of an argument indicating the benefits of America's space program. Your reason for using the syllogism is to suggest that Congress should increase NASA's long term appropriations. Your purpose, therefore, involves advocating more money for the program while the syllogism itself argues deductively that the United States benefits from such a program. Your thesis statement might look something like the following: "Because the United States benefits from the space program, Congress should consider increasing NASA's appropriations." Whichever method you choose, make sure your thesis is effective and supports your precise purpose.

A good deductive argument is a **sound argument,** that is one whose premises are all true and whose form is valid. The reader must be satisfied with both before he can give assent to the conclusion. The fact that an argument is valid does not make it automatically acceptable because the premises may be false. For example:

Major Premise All college students must take American history.
Minor Premise You are a college student.
Conclusion You must take American history.

This argument/syllogism is valid in the sense that if the premises are true, the conclusion necessarily follows; remember that validity is about the connection between the premises and the conclusion. The problem here, however, is that the major premise is untrue. (American history is a Texas state requirement for a college degree.) This argument, then, would be classified as valid but not sound.

When you are evaluating a deductive argument, ask yourself two questions:

1. Is it valid? Is the connection between the premises and the conclusion logical?
2. Are the premises true?

If your answer to both questions is "yes," the argument is **sound.** If your answer to either question is "no," you have a basis for rejecting the argument. The fact that the argument is unsound, however, does not mean that the conclusion is false; it simply means that the logic of this particular attempt to prove the conclusion has failed.

Inductive Reasoning

Induction is a less strict form of argument than deduction. The writer of an inductive essay aims to set forth evidence so that if the premises are true, the conclusion **probably** follows as true. Yet it is possible for the premises to be true and the conclusion false. Induction is often used in science, history, and everyday life when one cannot obtain enough evidence to make the conclusion absolutely certain. An inductive argument is **strong** when the writer has succeeded in the aim of arranging premises so that if they are true, the conclusion probably follows. Here are some examples of strong inductive arguments listed by type:

1. Generalization
   Mockingbird #1 was observed to eat worms.

   Mockingbird #2 was observed to eat worms.

   Mockingbird #99 was observed to eat worms.
   Conclusion: All mockingbirds eat worms.
2. **Prediction:** In the past, an increase in stock prices has been followed shortly by a decrease in bond prices. Stock prices increased last week.
   Conclusion: Bond prices will decrease this week.
3. **Analogy:** The car I am now driving weighs 3500 pounds, has a fuel-injected V-8, has

wind resistance coefficient of .29, and gets 30 mpg on the highway. The car I am about to buy has the same characteristics.
Conclusion: The car I am about to buy will get 30 mpg on the highway.

4. **Causal Inference:** The old bridge that was here yesterday is not here today. It was inspected last month and was found to be dangerously weak. We have had torrential rains for the past week, and the creek has risen up to a level above the roadway on the bridge.
Conclusion: The old bridge was probably swept away by the floodwaters in the creek.

In addition, a cogent inductive argument is one which is strong and whose premises are all true. When you are evaluating an inductive argument, ask yourself two questions:

1. Is it strong? Is the connection between the premises and the conclusion logical?
2. Are the premises true?

If your answer to both questions is "yes," the argument is **cogent.** If the answer to either question is "no," you have a basis for rejecting the argument. Once again, finding that an argument is not cogent does not mean that the conclusion is false; it merely means that this particular attempt to prove the conclusion has failed.

Evidence for Argumentation

The difficult part for the writer using inductive reasoning is to know whether he or she has sufficient evidence from which to draw a conclusion. All the writer can do is establish as high a degree of probability as possible. Once the writer is certain that the evidence provided for the inductive argument is sufficient, random (there are a variety of examples), accurate, and relevant, the writer must make what is known as the "inductive leap," a conclusion he or she reaches based on the evidence discussed. Unless the evidence meets these criteria, the argument will not be convincing and the writer will appear to have jumped to a conclusion.

If in developing evidence for an inductive argument, you discover an exception to your proposition, you should include it, too, in your discussion. A couple of reasons suggest this course of action. One, the inclusion of the single exception (negative evidence) can work to your advantage psychologically and ethically since, by including the exception with your evidence, you suggest to your reader that you are trustworthy in reporting such potentially damaging evidence. Second, you can take the opportunity to mitigate the force of the exception.

Kinds of Evidence or Support for Argumentation

Facts. Information widely accepted and repeatedly documented as objectively real constitutes the basis of inference; however, what constitutes a "fact" may be open to discussion. Be sure to distinguish between **fact, opinion,** and **judgment.**

Examples. Examples are used to support generalizations. They give specific instances to illustrate the material from which inductive generalizations are derived. Examples should be **relevant** and **appropriate.**

Authorities. Authorities are experts in various fields. Their work or statements are used as evidence to support claims. An authority may be an expert by virtue of his knowledge, skill, experience, training, or education.

Statistics. Numerical data in the form of tables, graphs, or charts are used to support claims. Since contradictory conclusions can be drawn from the same data, especial care must be taken in evaluating statistics. Good statistical data is usually presented visually (as a chart or table) as well as numerically; it should be accompanied by an analysis, and the source of the data should be clearly stated.

Public Records. Information drawn from public records, such as the Bureau of the Census, state agencies, or historical archives is frequently used as evidence.

Interviews. Personal interviews with people with experience can also be used as evidence, either as examples or as expert testimony.

Personal experience. If one has relevant personal experience, it can also be used as evidence as example or testimony.

Sources

Since a crucial element of persuasive argumentation is the evidence you use to support your assertions, you must pay particular attention to the sources of that evidence. Ask yourself: "Is the source reliable, unbiased, authoritative?" Sources include reports in the media, statistics, testimonials, research, and authority. More weight is generally attributed to primary sources than to secondary sources. **Primary sources** include such things as original documents and eyewitness accounts.

Secondary sources are those materials that are based on primary sources. For example, in a political science class you might be asked to write a paper on the freedom of religion in this country. One of your primary sources might be the Constitution itself; your secondary sources might include analyses and explanations of what the Constitution means by historians, scholars, and legal experts. Secondary sources should be assessed in relation to whatever primary evidence is accessible. You will find that among secondary sources there is usually disagreement, which makes your task of assessing them more difficult. Nevertheless, the more secondary sources you are able to accumulate, the better your chances are at arriving at some general assumptions regarding the general validity of your sources.

Common Logical Fallacies

A fallacy is a particular kind of defect in an argument, attributable to unsound and incomplete reasoning. It weakens an argument and makes it vulnerable to attack. Not only should you be familiar with the common fallacies so you can avoid them in your own argumentative essays, you *should* also be able to identify your opponent's defective arguments, allowing you to refute his assertions more easily. The following list includes a few of the most common fallacies in student argumentative essays.

Hasty Generalization. An argument that draws a conclusion based on insufficient or inappropriate samplings: "My Oldsmobile is a real lemon; therefore, General Motors manufactures inferior automobiles." "Students at the University of Houston are rude. Last night the guys in the room next to mine played their stereo at full blast until two in the morning, and as I was on my way to class this morning a bicyclist almost ran me down."

Red Herring. In hunting, a strongly scented object drawn across a trail will distract hounds and cause them to follow the new scent. In argument, a red herring is a different issue raised to lead attention away from the issue being debated or argued. Usually the new issue arouses an emotional response that creates a digression. "According to the newspapers, sexually transmitted diseases are climbing at an alarming rate among children in their teens. This raises a serious question about the wisdom of teaching sex-education in middle school."

Begging the Question. An argument based on an assumption that has yet to be proven: "The immoral experimentation on animals for research must be abolished"; "My narrow-minded English instructor seems to have forgotten how difficult it is to be a student."

Either/or Reasoning. An argument that suggests that only two alternatives exist when more than two actually exist. "If you quit college, you will never succeed in anything you do." "We can recognize that athletes who participate in major sports must be given special consideration at Texas A&M, or we can let the university sink into athletic oblivion."

Faulty Analogy. An argument based on a comparison of two things that share few or no common and relevant features. An analogy should be carefully examined to be sure that the things being compared are alike in ways essential to the conclusion being drawn. The fact that they are alike in some ways is not enough. "Since he was a good actor, I'm sure he will make a good President." "Bill, you are a superb computer technician. You seem to have a natural talent for analyzing system problems and remedying them. Surely, then, you should be able to analyze the problems in the rough drafts of your papers and turn them into polished essays."

Argumentum ad Hominem. The Latin phrase means *argument against the man* and names the fallacy of attacking the person rather than his argument. Such an attack may be legitimate when someone presents no argument but his own unsupported testimony. For example, the procedure is frequently used in courts to impeach witnesses who are testifying as experts. If it can be shown that they are not experts or that their testimony cannot be relied on, their trustworthiness as witnesses is seriously challenged. However, if someone presents evidence to support a claim, simply attacking his character is illegitimate. "Mr. Grumpky should not be allowed to serve on the school board because he is a non-Christian." "I went to a meeting on gender issues last night. The speakers were about as homely a group of women as I've ever seen. No wonder they hate men. Maybe if they dressed a little better and put on some makeup they wouldn't have to be concerned about gender issues."

Argumentum ad Populum. This "appeal to the people" is used particularly by politicians and advertisers. This fallacy ignores the issue at hand to appeal to the in-group loyalties and fears of the audience. Appeals to prejudice and self-interest are also part of this appeal. For example, one might argue that people should be against any form of government regulation of business since America was founded on the principle of freedom from oppression.

Appeal to Ignorance. This argument implies that since no one has proved a particular claim, it must be false; or, since no one has disproved a claim, it must be true. This fallacy usually involves a matter that is either incapable of being proved or has not yet been proved. "Since no one has convincingly disproved Darwin's theory, it must be valid."

Tokenism. This fallacy occurs when one makes only a token gesture (does very little of what is required), but then shouts or brags about it as loudly as one can. For example, a company might point to a highly placed executive who is female to show how well they treat and promote women when, in fact, she is the only woman in an executive position in the whole company.

The Straw Man Fallacy. This fallacy occurs when a person misinterprets or distorts an opponent's position to make it easier to attack, or when he attacks weaker opponents while ignoring stronger ones. For example, when opponents of gun control characterize those who are for some limitations on the ownership and use of weapons as radicals who would do away with hunting and Americans' constitutional right to bear arms, they are attacking a straw man.

Bandwagon fallacy. An argument that claims that something cannot be true (or false) because a majority of people support (or oppose) it. Based on popular opinion, the argument appeals to prejudice and ignores the facts. For example, it is obvious that any caring parent would not want his/her child attending school where a classmate has HIV.

Slippery Slope. An argument based on an unlikely chain reaction; it rests on an alleged chain of events, and there is not sufficient reason to believe that the implied effect will actually occur. For example, "If we legalize marijuana, the United States will become a nation of addicts and criminals." (If ... then ...)

Selective Sampling. Proof offered that contains part of, but not the whole truth. Since not all the facts are stated, the claim can be true and false (misleading?) at the same time (half-truths). For example, "Three out of five dentists surveyed preferred Brand X toothpaste."

Unreliable Testimony. An argument based on an untrustworthy, biased, or unqualified authority. (Fame/celebrity doesn't qualify as authoritative or expert opinion). For example, "Several of my neighbors support the termination of our school's head coach."

Circular Reasoning. An argument based on the repetition of an assertion as a reason for accepting it: "Drugs are harmful because they injure the body." "The president would never lie to the public because he is an honest man."

False Cause. An argument that confuses a causal relationship. For example, one might mistake a contributory cause for a sufficient one, or assume that because one event occurred before a second event, the first caused the second (an example of the **Post Hoc, ergo Propter Hoc** fallacy, a Latin phrase meaning *after this; therefore because of this.*) "Because the city council outlawed firearms, the crime rate declined." "Research shows that successful people have large vocabularies; therefore one way to become successful is to develop a large vocabulary."

Parts of an Argumentative Discourse

In his *Rhetoric,* Aristotle discusses the five parts of the deliberative discourse (a discussion of what we should or should not do to bring about some future goal), only two of which, **invention and disposition,** are relevant to the organization of the written essay.

Invention. Invention is the process or method writers use to discover arguments. Aristotle divided the process into finding arguments and devising arguments from scratch:

Non-artistic proofs are arguments you discover that have already been formulated by others. We call this process research. For methods of developingnon-artistic proofs, see your handbook on research strategies. **Artistic proofs** are arguments you develop yourself.

a. Pathos: Emotional Appeal
b. Ethos: Ethical Appeal
c. Logos: Logical Appeal
You will be expected to use the logical appeal in your essay, to avoid overly emotional appeals, and to incorporate the ethical appeal throughout. **Topics** are proofs grouped under common headings. Under common topics Aristotle discusses such topics as definition, comparison-contrast, causal analysis, and the proper use of testimony or authority. See *Chapter Three* for detailed discussions of these methods of exposition. Under specific topics for deliberative discourse, Aristotle points out that the purpose of an argument is to persuade the reader that your solution to a particular problem is logical and just and that it will benefit him in some way. These are the twofold goals of your argument.

Disposition. Disposition is the way one disposes or organizes one's arguments.

According to Aristotle, there are six parts to the disposition of an argument: **Introduction.** In your introduction you need to supply an attention-getting opener to your topic and a statement of your proposition/claim (the stand you intend to take). **Narration.** The narration is a discussion of the background of the issue under consideration. Readers, for example, may not know that there is a problem to be solved. The amount of background material you provide depends upon the knowledge of your audience and the complexity of the issue you are dealing with. **Division.** In the division you list the arguments you will advance in support of your proposition/claim. **Confirmation.** The confirmation is the longest and most important part of your argument. Here you give the evidence to support your proposition/claim arranged in the order you have listed in the division.

Refutation. The refutation is a discussion and rebuttal of your opponents' counter arguments. See below. **Conclusion.** In your conclusion make a strong appeal for acceptance of your argument.

Refutation

In a face-to-face argument, we have the advantage of responding directly to an opponent. In writing, however, we lack this advantage. Therefore, we must depend on **refutation** when we argue our ideas in writing. In your refutation, you take your opponents' arguments and prove they are, to some degree, wrong, invalid, or fallacious. Methods of refutation include pointing out an opponent's faulty premise, an error in deductive logic, a deficient definition, a logical fallacy, any inappropriate or inaccurate evidence, or a questionable authority, to name a few. For the most part, refutation involves undermining an opponent's argument. You might deny his proposition, showing that you cannot both be right. You might refute the truth of his premises or object to the inferences drawn from the premises, saying, in effect, "I admit the truth of your premise, but I challenge its validity in this particular instance because...." Or you might undermine your opponent's insufficient evidence for such an argument. Let good judgment and common sense rule. Consider your audience and his or her emotional biases, the occasion, the subject, and your own personality to help you determine the best course of action regarding refutation.

Some instructors prefer that you refute the opposition before beginning your confirmation. There is reasonable cause for such placement, especially if your opponents' views are shared strongly by your audience. However, if your opponents' arguments are weak, you can afford to delay refutation until the end of your own argument, using your discussion to build a case against your opponents' views. If your audience is hostile to your views, it might work to your advantage, psychologically, to delay your refutation until the end of your argument, to keep the direct attack of your opposition out of sight as long as possible. You need not remind your audience at the outset of your opposition, thus closing their ears to the remainder of what you have to say. By placing the refutation at the end, you may dispose your audience momentarily to hear what you have to say without compounding their hostility. Finally, you can also incorporate refutation wherever it is needed in each paragraph, rather than placing it in a separate section.

Questions to consider when revising your argument essay:

1. Are your premises true? Will your implied premises be clear to your reader?
2. Did you check your premises and reasoning to make sure your argument is sound, true, and valid?
3 Did you make certain that your enthymeme's missing portion does not alter the argument?
4. Is your argument free of logical fallacies?
5. Is your representation of the facts for your argument honest and accurate?
6. Does your proposition or thesis statement say what you want it to say, and does it clearly indicate your purpose?
7. Is your tone consistent with your purpose, audience, and subject matter? Does it contribute to the development of your ethos?
8. Have you identified your audience and adopted the appropriate voice for your audience?
9. Did you use restraint with your emotional appeals? Are your emotional appeals appropriate for your audience and subject matter?
10. Is your argument supported with adequate and convincing examples?
11. Have you indicated your order or pattern of development, either by listing reasons (inductive) or premises (deductive)?

CHAPTER 7

Visual Rhetoric

We live in a visual world. Every day we are inundated with internet pop-ups, television commercials, billboards along the highway, and ads on MySpace. What you may not realize is that these ads are carefully designed to get you to feel, think, or act a certain way. In other words, all of these images use visual rhetoric. Before you can think about using visual rhetoric yourself to persuade an audience, the first step is to learn to "unpack" examples of effective visual rhetoric, or learn how to "read" a visual image. First, refer to the checklist:

A Checklist for Analyzing Images (Especially Advertisements)

- What is the overall effect of the design? Colorful and busy (suggesting activity)? Quiet and understated (for instance, chiefly white and grays, with lots of empty space)? Old fashioned or cutting edge?
- What about the image immediately gets your attention? Size? Position on the page? Beauty of the image? Grotesqueness of the image? Humor?
- What is the audience for the image? Affluent young men? Housewives? Retired persons?
- Does the text make a logical appeal ("Tests at a leading university prove that...," "If you believe X, you should vote 'No' on this referendum")?
- Does the image appeal to the emotions? Examples: Images of starving children or maltreated animals appeal to our sense of pity; images of military valor may appeal to our patriotism; images of luxury may appeal to our envy; images of sexually attractive people may appeal to our desire to be like them; images of violence or of extraordinarily ugliness (as, for instance, in some ads showing a human fetus being destroyed) may seek to shock us.
- Does the image make an ethical appeal – that is, does it appeal to our character as a good human being? Ads by charitable organizations often appeal to our sense of decency, fairness, and pity, but ads that appeal to our sense of prudence (ads for insurance companies or for investment houses) also essentially are making an ethical appeal.
- What is the relation of print to image? Does the image do most of the work, or does it serve to attract us and lead us on to read the text?

From: *From Critical Thinking to Argument: A Portable Guide*, p.94 by Sylvan Barnet and Hugo Bedau. © 2004 Bedford/St.Martin's

You can use the checklist to begin to understand why creators of not only advertisements, but other forms of visual media (such as music videos), made the decisions they did in choosing colors, fonts, layout and, of course, images. Using the checklist, examine some of the following examples of visual rhetoric and begin analyzing the images:

What's the first thing you notice about the "I Am Not a Nugget" image? The text? The colors? Can you guess who the target audience is for this image? If you guessed, kids, you are right. This is a popular form of visual rhetoric that can be found on the peta2.org and petakids.org websites. PETA, or People for the Ethical Treatment of Animals, actively targets young people in its pro-vegetarian and anti-animal cruelty campaigns. And guess what their target audience (kids) loves to eat...chicken nuggets at fast food restaurants, of course! Think about the colors, font selection and the overall design. In what ways would this be appealing to a younger audience? Now, think about what the ad is asking this audience to *do*. The ad anthropomorphizes (or humanizes) the chick by using the first person...the chick is speaking to the audience. What kind of response do you think this elicits? Emotional? Logical? If the kids think logically, they know that chicks can't really talk. By humanizing the cute chick, the ad may be successful in getting kids to think twice about ordering those chicken nuggets.

Sometimes ads rely on both logical and emotional appeals. Take, for example, this ad created by "Democracy Means You."

Think about how this ad uses symbols and allusions. When you read the ad, did you read "Osama heart your SUV," or "Osama *loves* your SUV?" You probably automatically inserted "love" for the heart symbol. Think about what the ad is trying to get across. Why would Osama bin Laden love our SUV's? You have to think logically to make the connection between terrorism and America's dependence on foreign oil, which is certainly not helped by gas guzzling SUV's. Would the ad make you feel guilty (an emotional reaction) for driving an SUV? Maybe, maybe not. But this ad may be working on a deeper level. What if the viewer of this ad consciously or subconsciously makes the connection to this earlier, more ubiquitous ad: "I Love NY".

Note how the ads are strikingly similar in their design and layout. It could easily be argued that the first ad is making an allusion to the NYC ad. What happens if the viewer of the "Osama loves your SUV" ad thinks about New York City, which was the main target of Osama bin Laden's terrorists? Now do you think the ad would be successful in provoking an emotional response?

Here's another example of visual rhetoric that relies even more heavily on allusion to make an argument. This image appeared on the cover of the April 28, 2008 edition of *Time* magazine:

The cover is, of course, alluding to the famous image of the marines raising the American flag on the island of Iwo Jima during World War II. Based on this, how does this piece of visual rhetoric ask Americans to view global warming? The cover also offers a cautionary tale. Some veterans were offended by the ad and wrote angry letters to the editors of *Time* and other publications. Sometimes visual rhetoric can evoke an emotional response other than what is intended.

Now that you've seen some examples of visual rhetoric and thought about how choices about colors, symbols, design, and allusions all can impact how your audience responds, begin thinking about how you can translate an argument, either written or oral, into a visual piece. If you were to choose a symbol for your argument, what could it be? Think carefully about the color choices you make. Do you want to use red to symbolize love and valentines, or red because you want to evoke images of blood and gore? What about font selection? Do you think using **this kind of font would be appropriate for a logical appeal that is targeted at an audience of** scientists? How can you make allusions that your audience will relate to? For a list of other rhetorical devices and the definition of each, refer to Robert Harris's website, Virtual Salt at http://www.virtualsalt.com/rhetoric.htm

CHAPTER 8

Research & Using Sources

Getting Started

In the United States, we benefit from the centuries-old tradition of free access to information.

Traditionally, libraries have been places where individuals could locate data and texts on almost any topic. Indeed, the concept "library" means collections of texts and other materials. Because of open libraries, one did not have to be rich or powerful to have access to information. People of modest means could examine books and other materials they could not afford to purchase. Today, the development of computers and the Internet have vastly extended the idea of free access to information.

Today is a great time to be a college student researcher. Information from around the world is available with a few clicks of a computer mouse. The list of resources is virtually endless: email, computerized card catalogs, library databases, Web sites, and so on. Entire companies exist to develop easier ways to find information.

Therein lies the problem—almost the entire knowledge base of human history is available through a computer. The amount of information is so immense that the most important skill for researchers is knowing how to access information.

Yes, you can find information by simply entering keywords in a library computerized catalog or World Wide Web search engine. You can find much more refined and appropriate information, though, if you have knowledge of ways to search more deeply. That is what this guide is about—how to use the tools available to find the information you want—quickly and efficiently.

Research Sources Professors Expect

You have been assigned a research paper or project. What does your professor expect of you?

First of all, that you understand the assignment: What specifically does your professor want you to research? Do you have instructions about what kinds of sources your professor wants? Are restrictions put on what Internet or database sources you can use? Possibly, your instructor has specified that you need to use books, journals, major magazines and newspapers, and certain Web-based information. This means that you are to use reputable sources to obtain a balanced, impartial viewpoint about your topic. So, how do you find these sources?

- **Books** College libraries collect scholarly books that are carefully researched and reviewed by authorities in the book's field. Look for recently published books rather than older books, even if they are on your topic. Locate scholarly books through the computerized catalog at your college (See Chapter 10: Campus Writing Resources).

- **Scholarly journals** Your instructor means peer-reviewed journals in which the authors have documented their sources. Your library should have print indexes to journals in which you can look up your topic. You may also be able to find journal articles—sometimes in full text—through the online databases offered by your college library. For example, try JSTOR: Electronic Journal Archive which offers full-text versions of more than 300 journals in a variety of fields or Academic Search Premier, which indexes more than 4,000 journals, magazines, and newspapers.
- **Major magazines and newspapers** You can locate full-text articles directly from the online versions of major print magazines and newspapers. Often, these publications charge a fee for articles not published recently. However, you can often find the same articles free through library databases.
- **Web-based information** Search engines provide access to Web sites with information on almost any topic. The problem with Web-based information, though, is that anyone with some knowledge of computers can put up a Web site on the Internet. Thus, information from Web sites must be carefully evaluated as to author, publishing organization, etc. (See section in this chapter on How to Evaluate Web Sources). One way to deal with this problem is to find Web information through the librarian-generated indexes and search engines which screen Web sites for credibility.

As you use the methods above to find sources for your paper or project, realize that your topic influences your choice of reference materials. If you are writing about a literary topic such as Shakespeare's *Othello*, you will find a number of relevant books and journal articles. If your topic is more contemporary, such as the current status of the Space Shuttle flights, you may be able to find some books or journal articles for background information, but you will need to use recent magazine and newspaper articles to find the latest information.

As you examine your sources, remember that gathering the information should help you discover what you think about your topic, not just what others think. This will enable you to create a paper based on your ideas and opinions, with source materials supporting your position.

Make a Research Plan

Will you be using the Internet simply as one research tool along with print texts? For many topics, some of the most current information can be found electronically, and it can greatly enhance your information collection. Will you be gathering all your information from the Internet? Not all topics have equal coverage on the Internet, but for many subjects (if your instructor agrees), you can collect everything you need without leaving your computer terminal.

When making a research plan, you need to consider your assignment. Does it say, "Write an argumentative essay about an environmental problem such as toxic waste or acid rain?" If so, you know you need to narrow the topic from the environment in general to a more specific topic such as toxic waste. Perhaps narrow it to an even more specific topic such as programs for nuclear waste disposal or the recycling of environmentally damaging substances. If you aren't sure what specific topic interests you, you will need to look first at some general sources about the environment to help you choose a topic. Several research resources on the Web can help you narrow a topic and then gather information about it.

Best Information on the Net

Resources by Major
Hot Paper Topics
Alphabetical Index

Student Resources
Faculty Resources
Online Reference Resources
Disability Resources
Current Events
Resources for Librarians
Library Home

Hot Paper Topics

Affirmative Action

Article Files and Indexes to Hot Topics

Attack on America / Terrorism

Bioethical Issues

Censorship

Death Penalty

Drug Issues

Enron

Gender Issues

Gun Control

Health Care Reform

Help for Term Paper Writers

Human Rights

Identity Theft

Internet Issues

Media Issues

Miscellaneous Issues

Nanotechnology

Plagiarism

Hot Paper Topics, http://library.sau.edu/bestinfo/Hot/hotindex.htm, collects librarian-screened Web sites on topics popular with college students.

For example, connect to Hot Paper Topics at http://library.sau.edu/bestinfo/Hot/hotindex.htm, and find links to references collected by librarians at the O'Keefe Library on popular paper topics such as affirmative action and school vouchers. Browse through the subject links, and you may find a topic that interests you. Then you can do additional research on the topic using other types of electronic resources discussed in this book.

RESEARCH STRATEGIES FOR FINDING ELECTRONIC SOURCES

1. Using a subject index, either in a search engine such as Yahoo! (page 83) or a librarians' subject index (page 88), browse sites in your general topic. See what kinds of information are available on what specific topics.
2. Check online media links for articles on your general topics (page 89).
3. Search one or more of your library's full-text periodical databases for your general topic and, through them, obtain journal and magazine articles (page 94).
4. Narrow your search to a topic specific enough to write about in the length of research paper you are assigned.
5. Use one or more keyword search engines to locate additional relevant sites (page 8 1). Repeat steps one to three for your specific topic.
6. Compile the resources you have identified into a working bibliography.

Once you have decided on a narrow topic, you can use other subject indexes, keyword search engines, full-text databases, and media links to find additional resources. As you locate resources, assemble them in a working bibliography, which will help you keep track of them as potential resources. Remember that research is a recursive process. As you explore sources, you may find yourself changing the narrow topic you have selected, and this will require you to find additional sources. Even when you reach the writing stage of your project, you still may need to locate information sources to fill holes in your argument. The research is not complete until the project is complete.

Evaluate Web Sources

Many people tend to believe what they see in print. They may think that if information is in a book or a news magazine, it must be true. If you read critically, however, you know that all sources must be evaluated. Does a source give a balanced reporting of the evidence, or does it display bias? What resource sources are cited? What authorities are utilized? With the Internet, perhaps even more than with print texts, it is important to evaluate your sources. Undoubtedly, much reliable and valuable information is published through the Web, and you should not hesitate to use sources that, in your judgment, are credible. Remember, though, not all information on the Web is accurate. Anyone with a Web connection and a little knowledge can create a site, and automated search engines will include that site in their databases. Also, many sites are commercial and may have their own marketing reasons for promoting certain information. Before relying on information, ask yourself the following questions listed in "How to Evaluate Web Sources."

You may intentionally study biased sources on the Web such as home pages of political candidates, special interest groups, or companies selling products. If so, do not take their information at face value.

Indeed, you can make your evaluation of biased texts part of your argument. You could, for example, compare what a company selling a health food supplement such as ginkgo biloba or omega 3 oils says about that product with what you read in your search of other texts related to that product (including scientific studies). One of the Web's revolutionary aspects is that individuals and organizations can put their side of the story directly before the public. It is part of your job as a Web consumer to evaluate critically the motivation or validity of these direct-to-the-public texts.

Use Computer Technology to Enhance Research and Writing

Today's Web-browsing and word-processing programs offer a number of features that can make your research collection, organization, and revising much easier than recording information by handwriting.

HOW TO EVALUATE WEB SOURCES

Who Is the Author?

An important first step in establishing credibility of a Web site is considering the authorship. Credible authors that publish on the Internet generally will give a brief statement of their qualifications, or they may post a resume. If your article was published in a magazine or newspaper, search the publication for other articles by the same author. If the author has an affiliation with a university, you can search the university's Web site for additional information about the author. You can also do a keyword search for that person through a search engine.

Who Is the Publisher?

The publisher often is as important as the author. If the text was published in a reputable journal, magazine, or newspaper, the credibility of the publication attaches to the article. If your text was published on a Web site, not a publication's Web site, you need to employ other methods to assess the credibility of the publisher.

If you found the Web site through one of the librarian-reviewed research engines (pages 87-88), for example, you know the site has been evaluated and found acceptable for academic use.

You may be able to tell if the Web site is linked to an organization by looking at the URL or Web address. The organization or company name in the URL, such as http://www.exxon.com indicates that the material is published on the Exxon Web site. The suffix of the URL is also helpful: .edu means an educational or research institution, .gov for government resources, .com or .net for commercial products or commercially-sponsored sites.

Does the Document Appear Professional?

Credible sources go through an editing and reviewing process. Does the text look balanced and fair? Watch for grammatical errors, punctuation errors, misspellings, and other errors that would have been caught during an editing process. Ask yourself whether the graphics of the site add to or detract from the authoritativeness of the site.

Does It Provide Information about Sources?

Look for a list of references at the end of the document and/or informal references-to sources in the text. Where did the author get his or her information? If you cannot tell where the information came from, why should you trust it? It is a good idea to choose a few of the references the author mentions and validate them by making sure that the books or journal articles used actually exist and are represented fairly.

Is It Current?

Look for a publication date or a "last updated" date. Most credible sources will have a date.-

Currency can also be checked by testing out the links on the page. Are the links still up-to-date and useable? Do the graphics or photos display?

What Is the Purpose?

Was the Web site created to offer trustworthy information, to persuade, to sell, or for some other reason? If the site is selling anything, use its content only with great caution.

Create Links to Your Sources with Bookmarks (Favorites)

Internet Explorer and other Web-browsing programs have a built-in feature to create bookmarks for pages you would like to return to in the future, and you can use this feature to create a folder of links for a particular research project. In Internet Explorer, bookmarks are called Favorites. Add a source to your list of Favorites by following these steps:

1. Direct your browser to the page that you want to add to your list.
2. Using the Favorites menu, click Add to Favorites.
3. When prompted, name the source.
4. Continue this process with other Web sources.
5. To open the link to a favorite source, use the Favorites menu, and click the page you want to open.
6. You can organize your list of sources by moving the links into subfolders. Using the Favorites menu, click on Organize Favorites.
7. When prompted, click Create Folder, type a name for the folder (perhaps the research topic), and then press ENTER.
8. Drag the links for sources in the list to the appropriate folders. Instead of dragging, you can also use the Move to Folder button instead.

"Cut and Paste" Text to Facilitate Note Taking

Like many other writers, you can use "cut and paste" computer technology to make note taking easy. For example, say you want to copy a section of a Salon article about recycling from the magazine's Web site:

1. Open a new document in Microsoft Word.
2. Display the text of your source in Internet Explorer.
3. Highlight a section of the text you want to save and use the Edit menu in Microsoft Word to copy the text. See the image on the next page that shows part of the article highlighted.
4. Paste the text into your Microsoft Word screen and put quote marks around the quoted text. Similar to the image below, add bibliographic information about the source to the top of the Word file and your own remarks about the quote.

You can continue to cut and paste sections of the article into the document and intersperse them with your own comments. Like the example in the image above, you may want to put quoted material in italics to distinguish it clearly from your own words. Later, you can convert quotes into summaries or paraphrases, if you wish.

RECYCLING IS GREAT -- UNLESS YOU LIVE CLOSE TO WHERE IT'S HAPPENING.

BY DAVID BACON | HUNTINGTON PARK, CALIF. --

recycling has an environmentally friendly image. Reusing the basic materials of everyday life to ensure a sustainable future for the planet has almost becomes God's work. It has also become big business, especially in places of enormous consumption and waste like Los Angeles.

Some 20 years ago, when L.A. drew up its master plan, the recycling industry hardly existed. Today industrial facilities that process glass, metal and concrete are mushrooming. But some people living in Los Angeles have a hard time seeing recycling's green image. Their problem? They live near the plants.

"There's always glass in the air here," complains Mercedes Arambula, whose home in the southeastern part of the metropolis is catty-corner from a huge Container Recycling facility. Mounds of broken glass rise to twice the height of an adult in the yard. Skip loaders constantly fill open truck trailers with it.

"I've lived here 18 years," she says. "My kids have asthma now, and my littlest one, who's 1 1/2, is always sick. I won't even let them play in the yard anymore. The trees around my house have all died anyway."

A neighbor, Ana Cano, wipes her finger across the dusty windshield of a parked van in front of her

It is easy to copy quotes from electronic articles by using "cut and paste" technology. Highlight the material to be quoted and select Copy from the Edit menu in Microsoft Word.

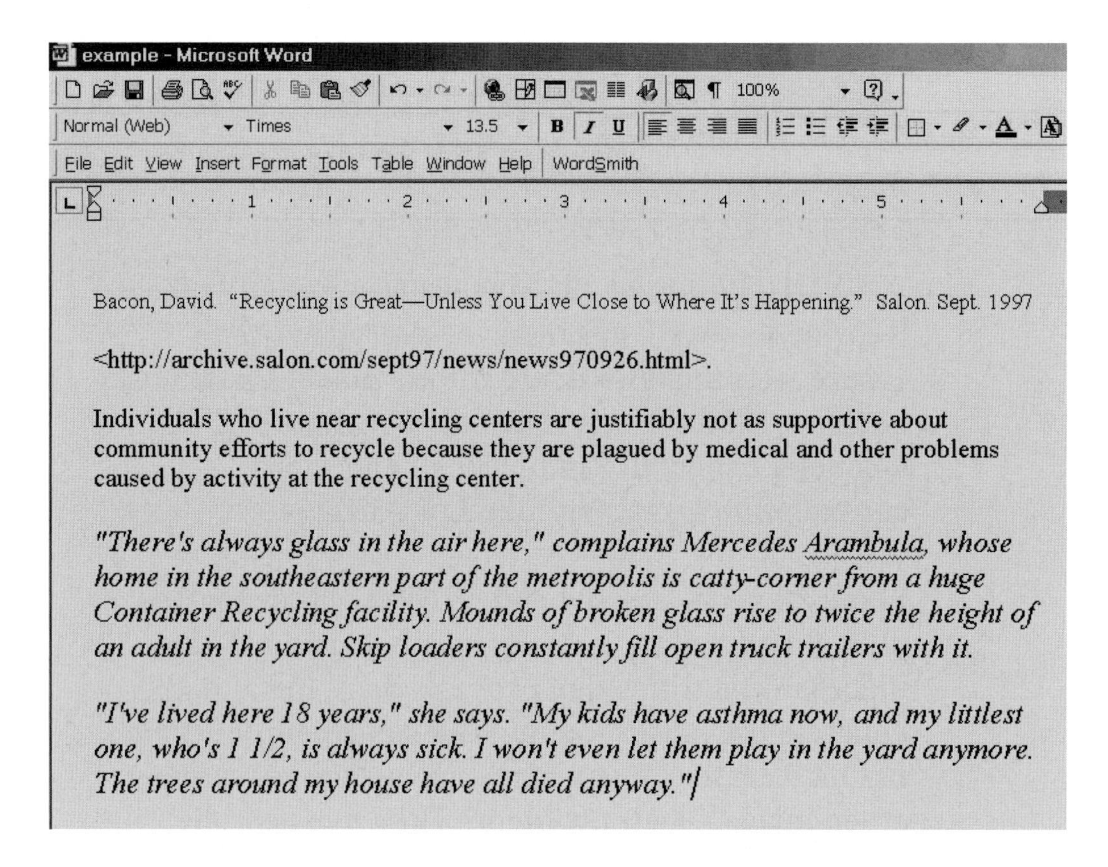

Paste the quote in an open Word document. Add bibliographic information and your comment about the quote.

Use Microsoft Word's Comment Feature to Label Quotes

One problem students often experience, when working with material from sources, is that source material is pasted as quotes into a draft, and information about the source can become lost or confused. If you use Microsoft's Comment feature to label each section associated with a particular source, that information is transferred when the wording is pasted into a new document. For example, if you were working on your notes about the Salon article (shown in the previous image), you can easily add bibliographic information about the source of the quote:

1. Highlight the portion of the text to be associated with the comment.
2. Go to the Insert menu and select Comment. In the box that appears below, type or cut and paste bibliographical information to be associated with that particular text. When you move the highlighted text to another document or a different location in a document, the comment will still be present and give bibliographical information. You can also use the Comment feature to ask yourself questions or leave suggestions for future revision. Windows XP utilizes the View menu and Markup feature to display Comments.

Use Email to Transmit Paper Drafts

Have you ever lost a draft of a paper or other assignment because the disk you used to save your document became corrupted, and your document would not open? Of course, you can have two disks and record each draft of your paper on both disks which would reduce the risk of losing a paper draft.

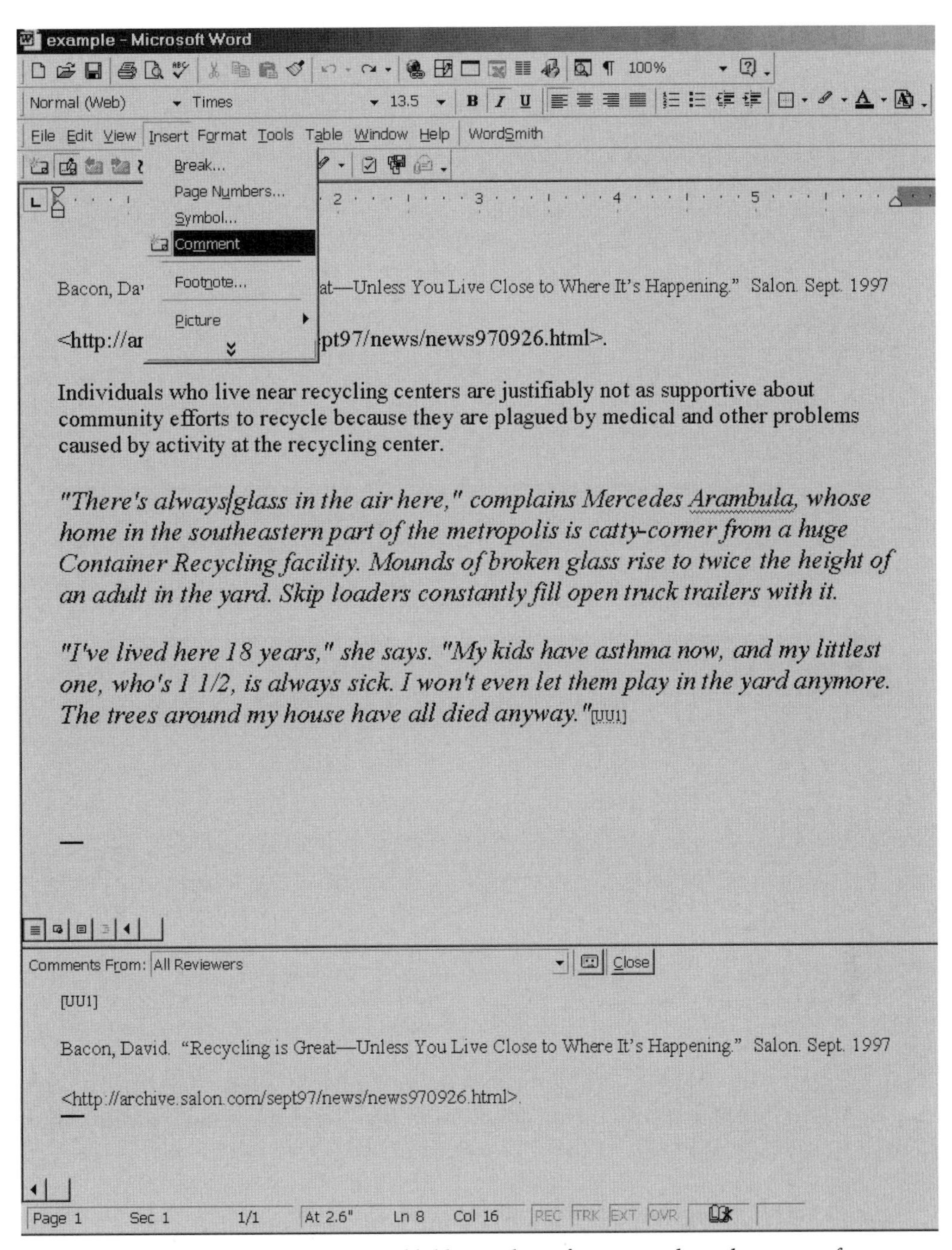

Use Microsoft Word's Comment feature to record bibliographic information about the source of a quote. Then, when you copy and paste the quote into your draft, the source information transfers to your draft document.

Another popular way to prevent the loss of your work is to email each draft to yourself as an email attachment. This second method has two advantages: If you are working on your paper both at home and at a computer on campus, you can transport the paper back and forth by email, eliminating the disk problem. Also, if you do not erase the emails containing your drafts as attachments, you have a record of each draft in case you want to retrieve text from an earlier draft.

Most email programs, such as Yahoo! Mail, allow you to easily attach a text file as an attachment. Simply display the compose message screen, usually by clicking on New Message or Compose Message, and

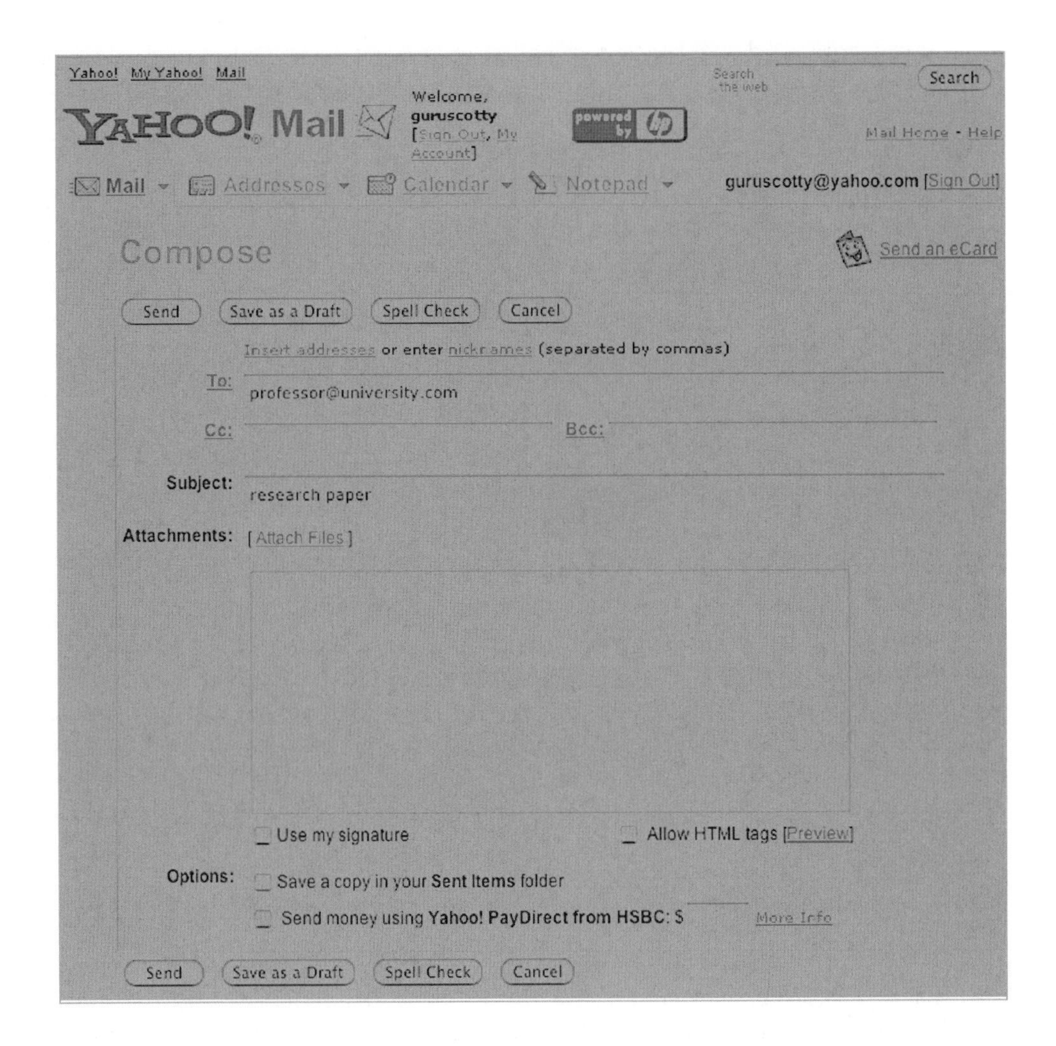

Yahoo! and other email programs allow you to easily attach files, such as paper drafts, and email them to yourself.

fill in the *To:* box with your own email address. Then click on *Attachments* and follow the program's instructions for attaching a file. Send the email, and it will appear in your email message inbox.

Locate Assignments and Join Discussions on Your Class Web Site

More and more professors are making use of Web-based technology to deliver all or part of a college course. On the simplest level, a professor may post a syllabus containing course policies and due dates on a Web page. At the most complex, a class is actually held in cyberspace, either in hybrid part-classroom/part-online format or completely online.

In many cases, the online course components may require a login and password to access materials. This policy restricts the use of the text, images, sound, and other types of files to the instructor and the students, thus protecting the professor's work and also allowing certain third-party copyrighted works to be included under the copyright "fair use" policy.

Your instructor may make use of course management software (CMS) such as WebCT or Blackboard to deliver the course content. The software allows instructors easily to post syllabi, assignments, and other files. In addition, CMS includes interactive features such as real-time chat rooms, email, and discussion boards that allow you to communicate with classmates and the instructor.

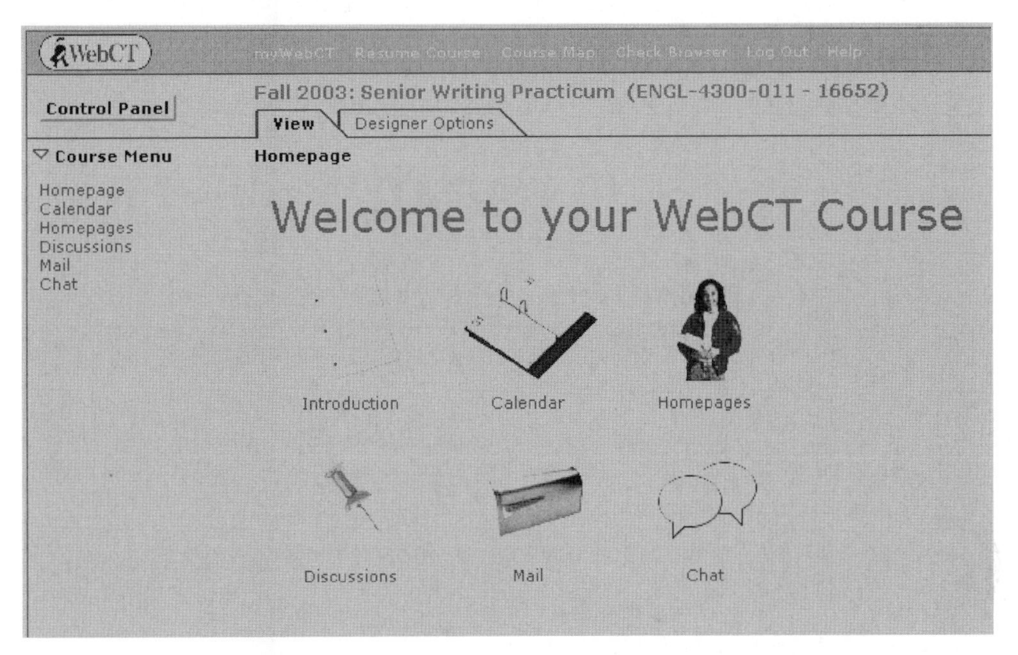

WebCT is a popular course management software used to deliver course content such as syllabi and assignments, as well allowing online class chat, email, and discussions.

Web Search Engines

The World Wide Web is an incredible resource for research. Through it, you can find full texts of pending legislation, searchable online editions of Shakespeare's plays, environmental impact statements, stock quotes, and much, much more. Finding the research sources you need, however, is not always easy. Research on the Web is far more than surfing. The Internet is immense, and its content is seemingly endless. For example, if you enter the word environment in one of the keyword search engines, you may receive thousands of "hits," or sites that relate to that topic from all over the world. How do you sift through all of that feedback in order to find information relevant to your topic? It is a problem that has not been completely solved on the Internet. However, some strategies will help.

Knowing how to use search engines to uncover data is an invaluable element of good research.

There are many search engines available on the Web, but they are not all created equal. Keyword search engines allow the user to search their database of indexed Web sites for keywords such as "dog" or "plasma." They return a list of results or hits, each of which includes a description, the URL (Web address) and the name of the Web site. Librarian-researched search engines and indexes provide links to sources which have been pre-screened for academic use.

Equal but Different: Try These Search Engines

Google (http://www.google.com) is the first search engine to consider. It is powerful and easy to use, with a crawler-based service, which means that the engine "crawls" the Internet looking for relevant Web sites. Google is everywhere; it has saturated the Web, integrating itself into every market. Indeed, anyone can add a Google search bar to a Web site.

To use Google, simply type in your search terms in the box and click on "Google Search." In the box below, the key words "First Amendment" appear in the box. Touch the button "Google Search," and the search engine will return a list of hits as shown on the next page.

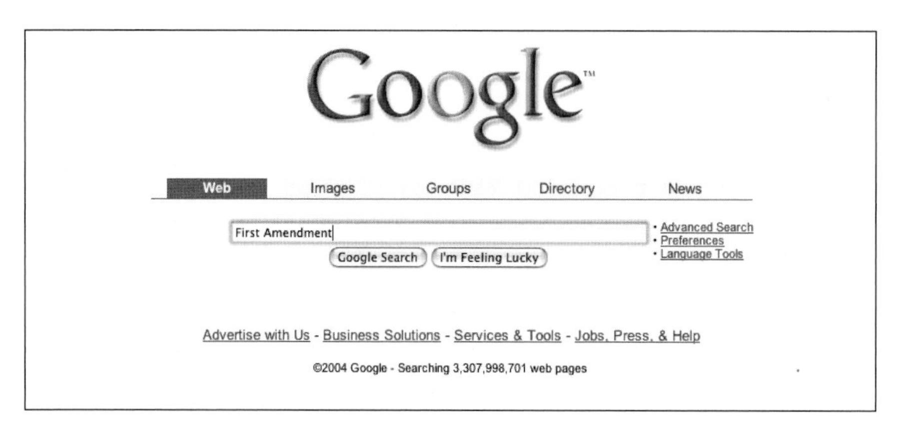

Google the most popular search engine, offers lots of features in addition to keyword searching.

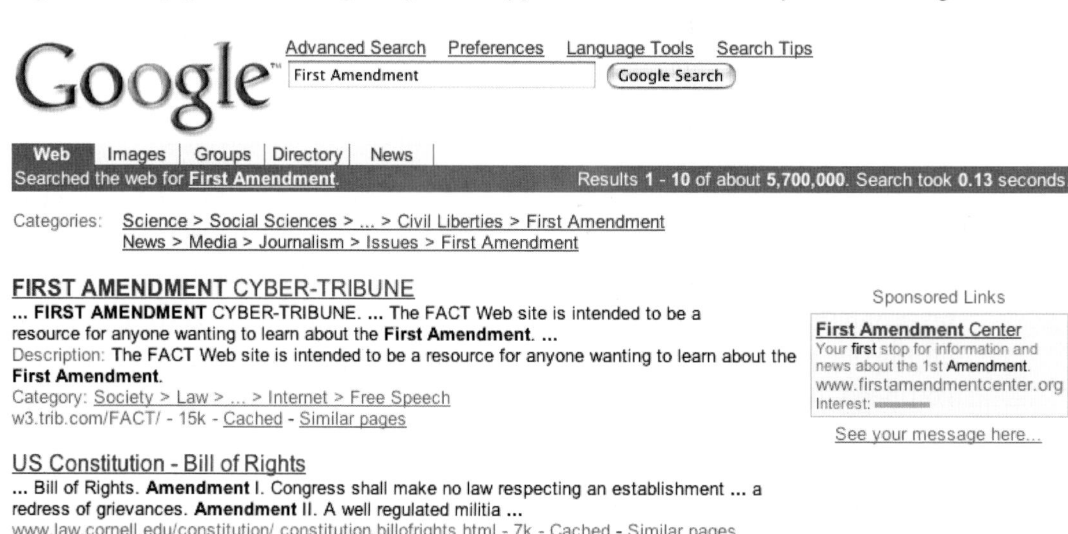

Above is the first part of a list of hits for the key words "First Amendment."

You can immediately see that an abundance of material is available on the First Amendment topic, including the original text of the amendment, fact sheets, and a link to the First Amendment Center.

For more information about how to optimize the Google search, read "The basics of a good search" at http://www.google.com/help/basics.html.

Google has a unique feature, the "Feeling Lucky" button which takes you straight to the hit Google thinks is most likely to fit your search criteria. Google also maintains cached copies of Web pages from when the sites were originally indexed by Google. Why would you want to look at a cached page? Web sites are updated so often that information you are using for research may be deleted before you finish your project. Go to Google's feature page and click on "Cached Links" to read more about cached Web pages. For more information about special features, read http://www.google.com/help/features.html.

Another excellent site for researching online is **Google Scholar™**. "Google Scholar™ provides a simple way to broadly search for scholarly literature. From one place, you can search across many disciplines and sources: peer-reviewed papers, theses, books, abstracts and articles, from academic publishers, professional societies, preprint repositories, universities and other scholarly organizations" (About Google Scholar™, Accessed 6-18-08). On this site you can find some full-text sources and some abstracted sources. The advantage over regular Google™ searching is that the sources cited are academic and reliable.

Yahoo! (http://www.yahoo.com) is an excellent keyword search engine. What also makes Yahoo! special is a separate search engine created and managed by humans that provides searches with a subjective view of the Internet. Access these human-selected sites by clicking on one of the subject headings from the Yahoo! main page.

Serious content only is here; the jokers, misinformers, and adult sites hoping to attract your business by misdirecting you to their Web sites have been edited out. But there are limits to the number of Web sites that can be reviewed by humans. Therefore, Yahoo! uses other methods—such as Google's crawler-based technology—to provide wider keyword coverage of the Internet.

Yahoo!, http://www.yahoo.com offers a keyword search engine, a subject directory, and free email.

Sample Search: Yahoo!'s Subject Directory

Suppose your instructor has asked you to write an essay about an environmental issue. You don't have a clear idea about a topic and decide to explore. Connect to Yahoo! (http://www.yahoo.com). Using the directory, examine the subject entry on the Environment and Nature under Society and Culture. You can click on any of the subtopics to receive a list of sites related to that subtopic. Or you can specify a search term in the box given for keywords (be sure also to click on the button that indicates to search only in that subcategory).

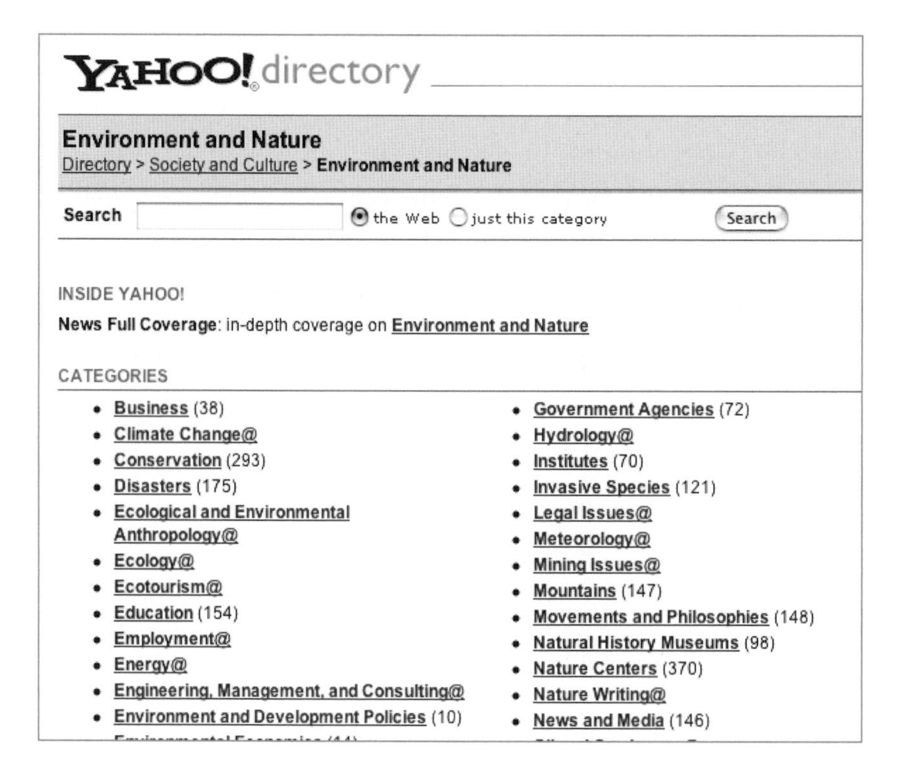

After browsing a number of the categories under environment and nature in Yahoo!, you may be able to narrow your topic, perhaps to Ecotourism, and then, even more specifically, to Eco Volunteerism.

Web Site Directory - Sites organized by subject   Suggest your site

Business & Economy
B2B, Finance, Shopping, Jobs...

Computers & Internet
Internet, WWW, Software, Games...

News & Media
Newspapers, TV, Radio...

Entertainment
Movies, Humor, Music...

Regional
Countries, Regions, US States...

Society & Culture
People, Environment, Religion...

Education
College and University, K-12...

Arts & Humanities
Photography, History, Literature...

Yahoo! offers a directory of human-reviewed Web sites by category on the home page. Choose a category and narrow your search by choosing a subcategory or do a key-word search in that category only, not in all of Yahoo!.

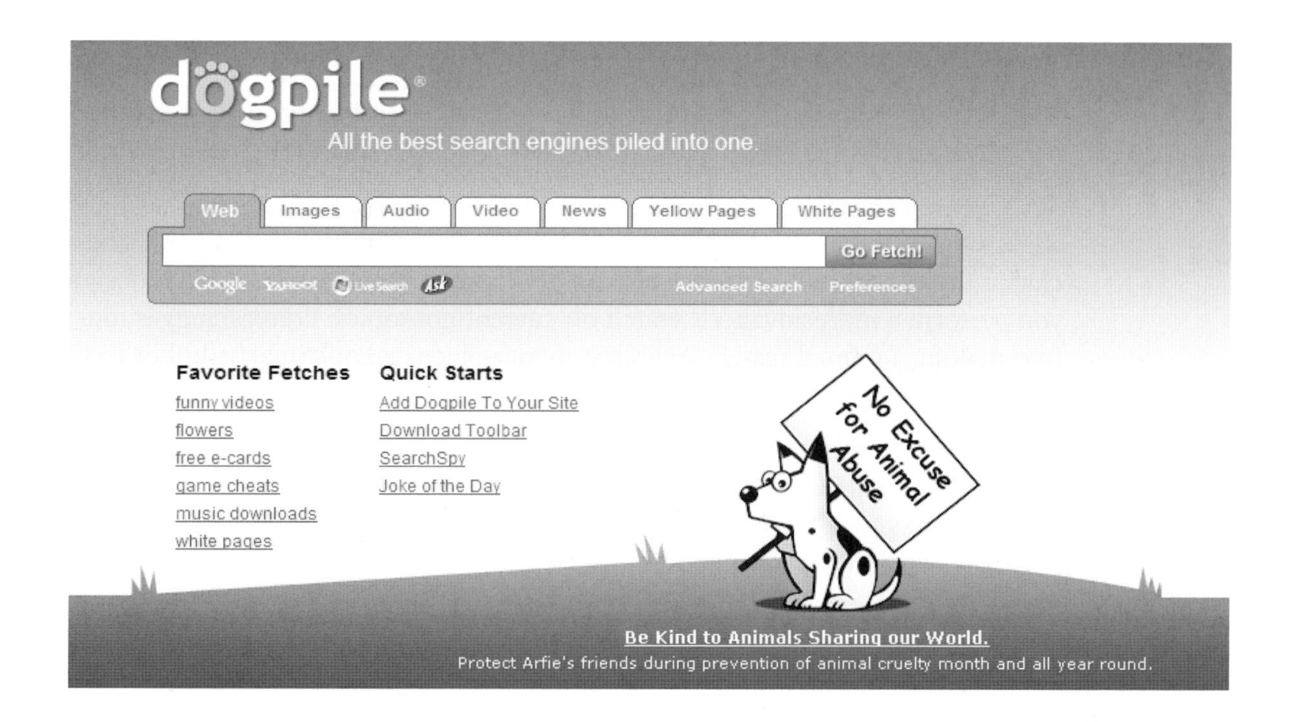

Dogpile is a metasearch engine which allows you to search several search engines at once.

Dogpile (http://www.dogpile.com)—despite the name—is a serious search engine. Their goal is, though, to be better than Google, the current ruling monarch of search engines. How do they plan to distinguish themselves and change the face of Web research? They claim to be a newer, perhaps better, metasearch search engine. Metasearch search engines pull results from several different keyword search engines, allowing the user to search more of the Web for results. Dogpile.com merges results from Google, Yahoo!, AltaVista, Ask.com, About, and LookSmart. Dogpile utilizes clustering technology, so results are given by category as well as in standard search format. It also clearly marks which links are commercially-sponsored, and users can request results by relevance or by search engine by simply clicking on a link. Try the Advanced Search features which offers several types of searches, including the use of Boolean operators (AND, OR, NOT). See also the box labeled "Tools: Refining Your Search" for a discussion of Boolean operators and other advanced search features.

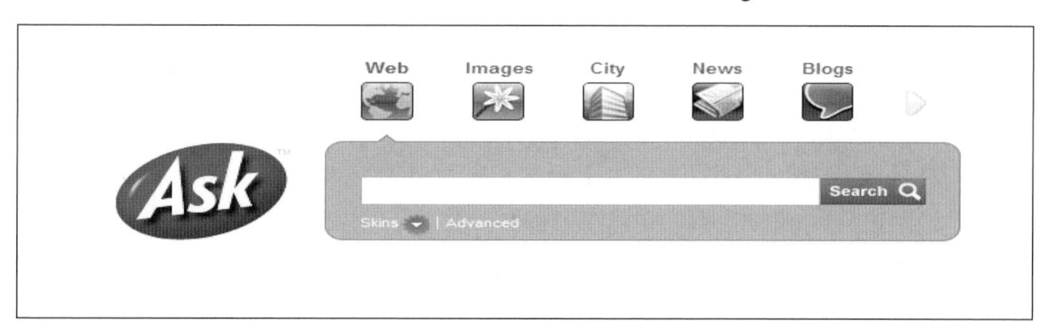

Enter search questions in plain language at Ask Jeeves.

Ask.com, (http://www.ask.com) allows you to enter a whole question rather than just key words. For example, you could ask questions such as "When is Mother's Day in 2010?" or "Who is Ray Bradbury?" Ask.com provides a researcher with a list of results to answer your question along with a "Related Searches" section providing results to searches similar to the question asked.

Other Search Engines to Try

AllTheWeb.com (http://www.alltheWeb.com). AllTheWeb is a crawler-based search engine and offers the option to search for news stories, images, and other file formats.

MSN Search (http://search.msn.com). Similar to Yahoo!, MSN Search has human editors who evaluate the most popular searches and choose sites for relevancy which are then included in the subject directory. It also has a "Popular Topics" section that is designed to help you perform a more advanced search on current hot topics. Editors' suggestions guide you into making a refined search. Search providers such as LookSmart add hits to the human-picked sites.

AOL Search (http://aolsearch.aol.com from within AOL and http://search.aol.com outside AOL). AOL users may prefer to use their built-in search engine, AOL Search, because it also provides links to content available only within AOL. A crawler-based engine, it also gives Web links in a manner similar to Google's.

Tools: Refining Your Search

All search engines provide advanced search features that allow you to enter more information than key words and, thus, narrow the search to filter out irrelevant sites. Here are some tips that work in most engines:

- Click on Advanced Search or Help on the search engine's main page. You will receive a dialog page that allows you to limit your search in a variety of ways including additional key words, language, and file format. For example, if you are looking for images, you can specify .gif, .jpeg, or other image file formats.
- Quote marks: Use quote marks around your search to limit results to words in a specific order grouped together. This tool is useful for searching for phrases or multiple word concepts such as "To be or not to be" or "dietary supplement." Most search engines will recognize two capitalized words in a row as a search string, such as Ray Bradbury or Star Wars.
- The plus sign (+) tells a search engine that all results must contain the word it precedes. For example, +Bush +Rumsfield would result in hits with both names.
- The minus sign (-) tells the search engine to ignore any results that contain a particular word.
- For example, Shakespeare –plays would return hits about other aspects of Shakespeare such as his poetry.
- Related searches: In most search engines, if you search for Shakespeare, you may be offered links to related searches such as Shakespeare's Sonnets, life of William Shakespeare, and the complete works of Shakespeare. These related search links generally appear near the top of a page of hits on a topic.
- Find Similar: Some search engines offer the option "find similar" following a hit of a link to similar pages.
- Search Within: Several of the major search engines, including Google, Lycos, and Yahoo! allow you to do a second search on the results of a first search. For example, if you search for "abortion" and receive too many hits, you can use the search within feature to search for a "third-term" within the hits you have already generated.
- Boolean operators—Use words such as AND, OR, and NOT to limit your search. For

example, if you use the keywords radioactive waste, some of the search engines will return hits for either radioactive or waste. If you type radioactive AND waste, however, the search engine will look for those two terms together. If you use the keywords Shakespeare AND NOT plays you will receive hits about Shakespeare but not his plays. Not all search engines recognize Boolean operators, however. You can find out which search engines support which terms at Search Engine Watch, http://www.searchenginewatch.com.

Librarian-Reviewed Indexes and Search Engines

One of the best ways for students to find Internet resources is through several indexing projects sponsored by major libraries. In the case of each index/search tool, librarians have personally reviewed and selected Web sites that are of value to academic researchers, including both students and faculty. These indexing Web sites may be organized by subject area, in addition to having keyword search engines. You might find it useful to bypass traditional search engines such as Google and Excite and to begin research for a term paper with these subject indexes. Thus, you might quickly locate the most authoritative Web sites without having to wade through masses of sites looking for the reliable ones. All of these engines are organized somewhat differently, so you might want to browse through them and select two or three that look user friendly to you.

Bub Link

http://bubl.ac.uk/link

BUBL features a subject index, in addition to a search engine, and offers a minimum of five selected resources for every subject indexed. It catalogs over 11,000 resources, carefully chosen in all academic disciplines, which increases each included site's credibility. The subject terms used are loosely based on the LCSH (Library of Congress Subject Headings) but have been adapted and expanded to make the subject index and search engine easier to use.

Hot Paper Topics

http://library.sau.edu/bestinfo/Hot/hotindex.htm

This site features librarian-researched links to credible sites for typical term paper topics such as attack on America/terrorism, bioethical issues, censorship, drug issues, Enron, gender issues, gun control, health care reform, human rights, and identity theft. See also the links on the "Best Info on the Net" Web site, http://library.sau.edu/bestinfo/Librarians/intergen.htm.

Infomine

http://lib-www.ucr.edu

Infomine is a librarian-built subject index and search engine designed for faculty, students, and researchers. It is divided into major collections: biological, agricultural, and medical sciences; business and economics; cultural diversity and ethnic resources; electronic journals; government documents; K-12 instructional resources; university instructional resources; internet enabling tools; maps and GIS; physical sciences, engineering, computer science, and math; social sciences and humanities; and visual and performing arts.

Internet Public Library

http://www.ipl.org

The Reference Center at the Internet Public Library divides Web resources into sections for arts and humanities, business, computers, education, entertainment, health, government, regional, science and technology, and social science. The "Ask a Question" section allows the user to send a query, and a real librarian will respond to questions generally in a few days. Connect to the "Ask a Question" Web page for instructions on submitting a question. The "Reading Room" provides access to standard reference texts such as almanacs, calendars, and dictionaries, as well as links to other Internet finding tools.

Internet Scout Project

http://scout.wisc.edu

The Internet Scout Project is not exactly a library project, but numerous librarians and educators are involved in its indexing. Sponsored by the National Science Foundation, the Internet Scout Project offers timely information to the education community about valuable Internet resources. Among its services is the searchable weekly Scout Report which features Web site reviews.

Librarians' Index to the Internet

http://lii.org

The Librarians' Index to the Internet prides itself for providing "Information You Can Trust." It is a searchable, annotated subject directory of more than 12,000 Internet resources selected by librarians for their value to students, librarians, and other researchers. Every site linked is reviewed at least twice before added to the Index, and the current inventory of links is reviewed constantly to eliminate dead links.

WWW Virtual Library

http://vlib.org

The WWW Virtual Library is the oldest human-screened index of Web sites. It was begun by CERN, the center for high-energy physics research where the Web was begun. Today, the WWW Virtual Library is organized and maintained by a group of volunteers. Organizations or individuals who have an extensive collection of links on a particular topic offer them to the library, and, if selected, a link is added to that collection. The library is quite extensive, and not all pages are located at CERN. The WWW Virtual Library does now also offer a keyword search option, in addition to the index.

Other Web Sources

Magazines and Newspapers

The New York Times, Time, Newsweek, and many other print publications offer full-text articles in special editions or complete Web versions of these print publications. Like other resources on the Web, several paths exist to reach these publications, including searching by publication title in a search engine. Generally, articles in these publications, however, will not show up in a keyword search unless you go directly to the magazine or newspaper and use the search feature.

Read today's news in many online newspapers and magazines. Using the publication's search feature, you can access recent articles for free. The publication may charge a small fee for articles in the archives, however. You can, though, locate an article in a publication's archive and copy the article's title, author, date, and page. For a free copy of the article, you can then locate it in one of your library's subscription databases (pages 94-97) or the library's periodical or microfilm sections.

Examples of Popular Newspapers and Magazines

New York Times
http://www.nytimes.com

HOME PAGE | MY TIMES | TODAY'S PAPER | VIDEO | MOST POPULAR | TIMES TOPICS

Get Home Delivery | Log In | Register Now

The New York Times

Tuesday, April 29, 2008 Last Update: 2:52 PM ET

Ameriprise Financial | NYT Archive Since 1981 | Search | Get Home Delivery | Personalize Your Weather

JOBS
REAL ESTATE
AUTOS
ALL CLASSIFIEDS
WORLD
U.S.
Politics
Washington
Education
N.Y./REGION
BUSINESS
TECHNOLOGY
SPORTS
SCIENCE
HEALTH
OPINION
ARTS
Books
Movies
Music
Television
Theater
STYLE
Dining & Wine
Fashion & Style
Home & Garden
Weddings/Celebrations
TRAVEL
Blogs

Saying Times Are Difficult, Bush Presses Congress to Act
By DAVID STOUT and ANAHAD O'CONNOR 51 minutes ago
The president called on Congress to expand energy production, stem the mortgage crisis and reduce what he called lavish subsidies to farmers.
· CNBC Video: Bush Press Conference on Economy

Consumer Confidence Slips as Home Prices Drop
By MICHAEL M. GRYNBAUM 5 minutes ago
American homes are losing their value at the fastest rate in two decades, a report said, while a confidence survey showed a growing gloom among consumers.

Obama Expresses Outrage at Former Pastor's Remarks
By THE ASSOCIATED PRESS 12

Iranian President's Visit Is a Test for India
By SOMINI SENGUPTA and HEATHER TIMMONS 12:53 PM ET
A visit by Mahmoud Ahmadinejad, seen arriving in New Delhi on Tuesday, gives India a chance to assert its independence from the United States.

SCIENCE TIMES »
Inside an Enigma
A trove of new photos provides a tantalizing look inside Iran's nuclear program.
· Interactive Graphic | Slide Show

Trial Opens for Hussein Aide; 28 Dead in Sadr City
By STEPHEN FARRELL 1:36 PM ET
Tariq Aziz went on trial in Baghdad as heavy fighting erupted between U.S. soldiers and gunmen in Sadr City.
· The Lede: Hussein's Execution Was Botched, Judge Says

MORE NEWS
· **Bush Discusses Report on Syria Strike** 1:16 PM ET
· **2 Construction Workers Badly Hurt** 8 minutes ago
· **Crisis Catches Up to Deutsche Bank** 24 minutes ago
· **3 Tornadoes Strike Virginia** 12:30 PM ET
· **Family Reunited in Austria Incest Case** 11:50 AM ET

ON THE BLOGS
· **The Caucus: McCain Describes Health Care Plan**
· **Dot Earth: Court Forces Action on Polar Bears**
· **The Lede: On YouTube, Decrepit Army Barracks**
· **DealBook: Who's the Hero in Mars-Wrigley Deal?**
· **Well: Parents' New Miley Problem**

MOVIES »
New DVDs
Early work from five women pioneers in filmmaking.

The Spirit of '68
The cinematic experiments of 1968 show how alive film can be.

Hard Lessons Learned
David Mamet finds inspiration in boxing.

OPINION »
· Herbert: Rev. Wright
· Brooks: Cultural Gap
· Op-Ed: Bad S.E.C. Reform
Post a Comment | Read (50)
· Editorial: Court Fumbles
Post a Comment | Read (243)

MARKETS » At 2:54 PM ET

S.&P. 500	Dow	Nasdaq
1,395.62	12,872.57	2,432.84
−0.75	+0.82	+8.44
−0.05%	+0.01%	+0.35%

GET QUOTES | My Portfolios »
Stocks, ETFs, Funds | Go

REAL ESTATE | AUTOS | JOBS | ALL CLASSIFIEDS

WHEELS
Mini's Instant Collectible
A special-edition Mini Cooper S from 2006, limited to 415 in the United States, could be a real collectible.
· The Wheels Blog

COLLECTIBLE CARS PHOTO GALLERY & EVENT CALENDAR »

SEARCH FOR NEW CARS
Select Make | Go
SEARCH FOR USED CARS
Select Make | Go
Advanced Search »

MORE IN AUTOMOBILES
· New Car Reviews

Web Links to Newspapers and Magazines

For links to magazines and newspapers, try this Web site:
Newsdirectory, http://www.newsdirectory.com

For magazines, look at these:
Magazines AtoZ.com, http://www.magazinesatoz.com

Yahoo!'s magazine list, http://dir.yahoo.com/News_and_Media/Magazines

For newspapers, try these:
Kidon Media Link, http://www.kidon.com/media-link

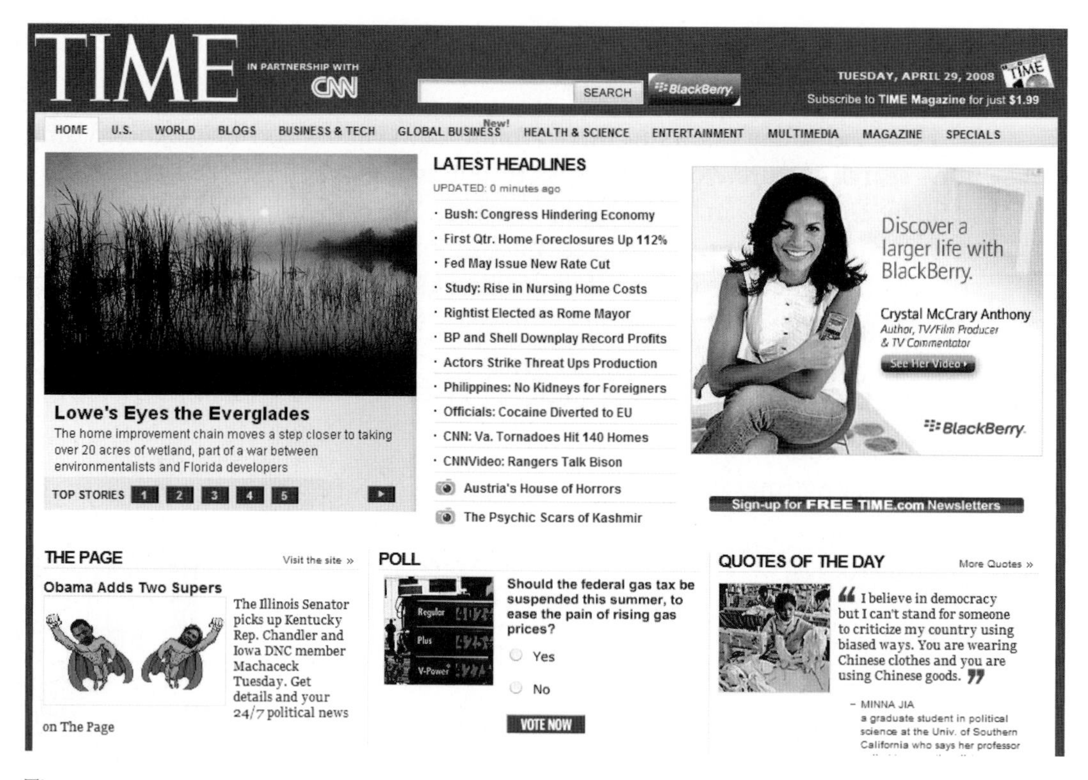

Time
http://www.time.com

Internet Public Library, http://www.ipl.org/reading/news

OnlineNewspapers.com, http://www.onlinenewspapers.com

Newspapers.com, http://www.newspapers.com

Yahoo!'s list,
http://dir.yahoo.com/News_and_Media/Newspapers

About Worldnewspapers, http://worldnewspapers.about.com/newsissues/worldnewspapers

Government Documents

Library Resources

Government documents present a wealth of information for many contemporary events and issues. Your library may be a federal depository, which means that users can locate many federal documents onsite. If so, you can look up government sources in the online library catalog. The screen capture below shows the result of a keyword search in a university's online catalog for information about the 2000 United States Census.

Your library may also have available online databases which provide full-text versions of government documents. These are two such databases:

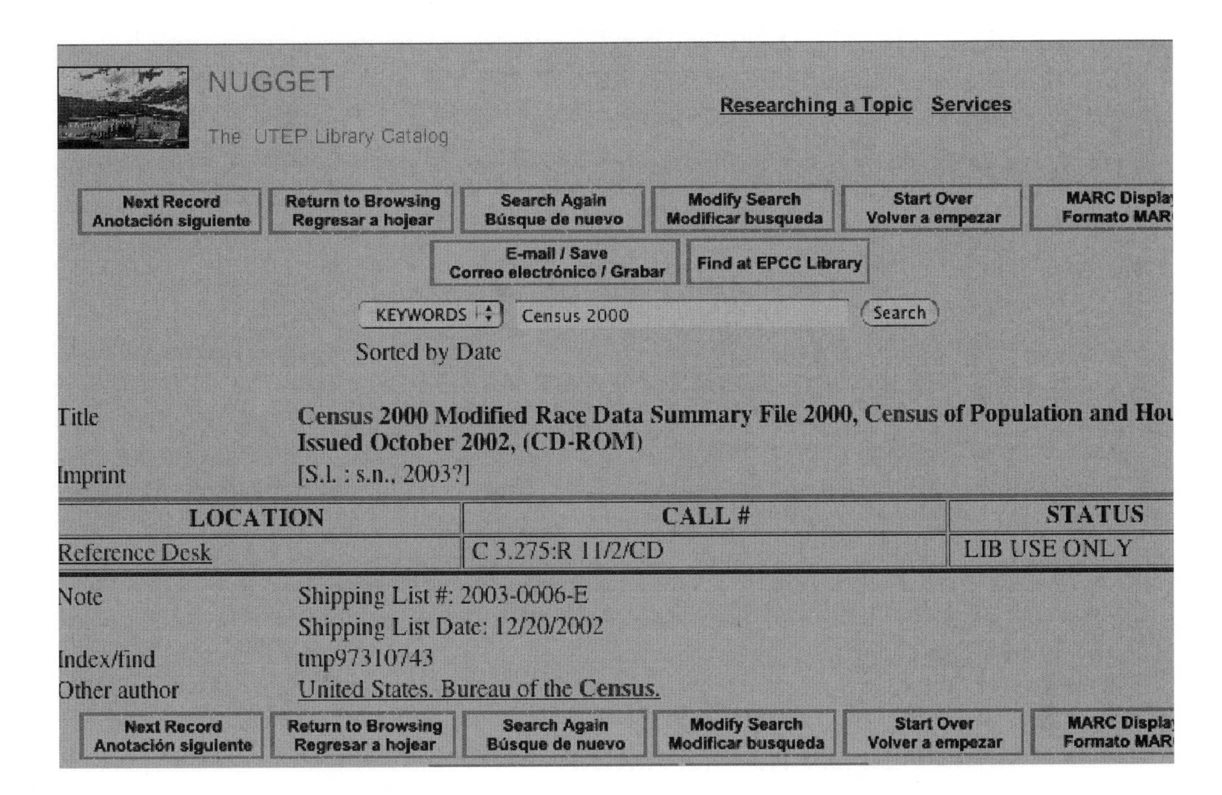

You can locate many government documents in your college library by doing a keyword search in your library's computerized catalog, if your library is a federal depository.

Lexis-Nexis Congressional Universe

Congressional Universe offers an index to congressional publications, including pending legislation, the Federal Register, and other documents dating back to 1970.

Lexis-Nexis Government Periodicals Universe

Periodicals Universe gives access to periodicals published by U.S. government agencies from 1987 to the present.

World Wide Web Resources

More and more government institutions and agencies now publish many of their documents on the World Wide Web. It certainly saves taxpayer dollars to do so, and it also makes documents more accessible to the general public. Try one or more of the gateway sites mentioned below.

FirstGov

http://www.firstgov.gov

The federal government provides FirstGov as an easy access point or "front door" which links to more 186 million Web pages from federal and state governments, most of which are not available through commercial Web sites. You can find, for example, everything from books in the Library of Congress to real-time tracking of a NASA space mission. FirstGov even offers a special Web page that collects information for students about financial aid and careers.

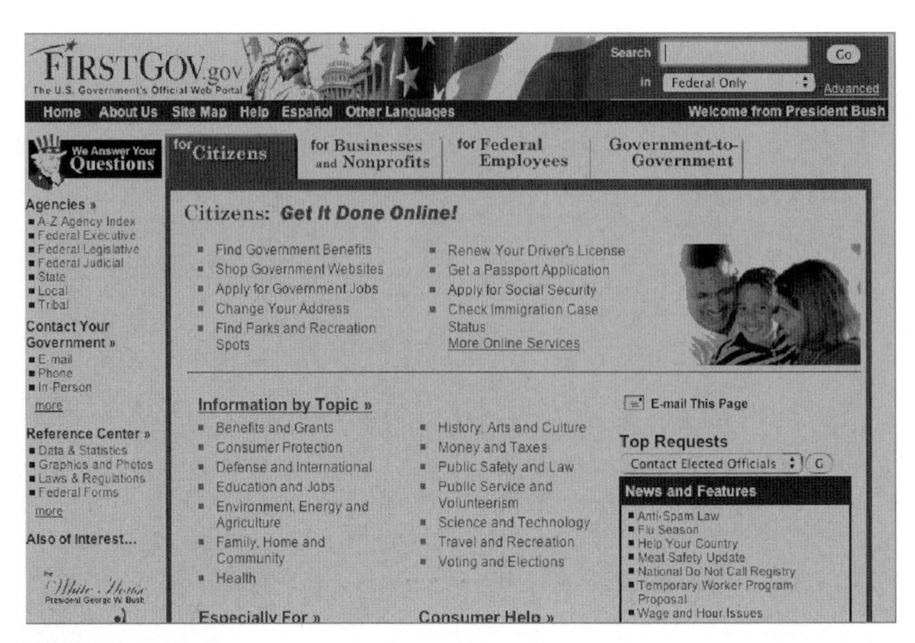

FirstGov

http://www.firstgov.gov

Thomas Legislative Information

http://thomas.loc.gov

This link provides information about pending legislation and other matters relevant to the United States Congress. It offers a full text of the *Congressional Record*, public laws since 1973, committee reports, and much more.

Federal Information Center

http://fic.info.gov

The Federal Citizen Information Center (FCIC) supplies answers to questions about consumer problems and government services. For example, if you want to know more about social security benefits, you can find a jargon-free explanation at this site. Also, it offers "before you buy" information about consumer products, as well as a list of the best places to send a consumer complaint.

The Federal Web Locator

http://www.infoctr.edu/fwl

The Center for Information Law and Policy offers this gateway to federal agencies and institutions, in addition to non-government federally-related sites.

Core Documents of the United States

http://www.access.gpo.gov/su_docs/dpos/coredocs.html

The Government Printing Office (GPO) maintains a digital collection of the basic federal government documents that "define our democratic society." The collection includes the Constitution, the Bill of Rights, landmark Supreme Court decisions, the Budget, the Census Catalog, and the US Government Manual.

Organizations and Corporations

One of the great benefits of the Internet is that you can gather information about an organization or corporation directly from its Web site without having the information filtered through the news media. You can learn about Greenpeace's campaign to save old-growth forests or Enron's amended Chapter 11 petition through their respective Web sites, for example. Remember though, you will read only about the corporation's or organization's side of the story, and when you include material from these or similar sites in a research project, you should acknowledge the source clearly, so your audience will know the information may be biased.

Read about Greenpeace's programs and protests directly on the Greenpeace Web site, http://www.greenpeace.org.

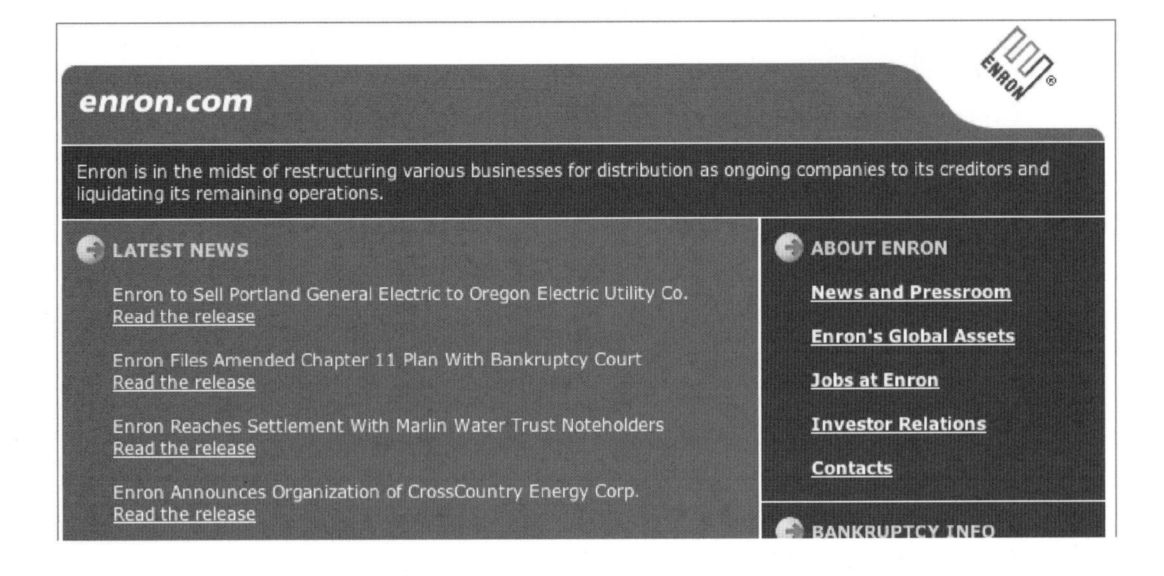

Read about Enron's corporate restructuring on their Web site, http://www.enron.com.

Library Tools

Library Computerized Catalogs

A library computerized catalog provides bibliographical information about the library's collection.

Likely, you can find call numbers and other essential location information about thousands of books, photos, videos, journals, and other items. Generally, catalogs can be accessed by keyword, subject, author, title, and call number.

On the library home page, you will find links to other information and services such as database searches, interlibrary loan, and course reserves.

Types of Searches

- Keyword—Unless you know the author or title of a book, keyword is the best type of search because it finds the search word or words anywhere in the bibliographical citation.
  Example: water quality
- Title—Type the exact order of words in the title.
  Example: History of the United Kingdom
- Author—Type the author's name, putting the last name first. You don't need to include a comma.
  Example: Miller Henry J.
- Subject—Type the exact Library of Congress subject heading.
  Example: Spanish language - Grammar, Historical
- Call Number—Type the exact call number.
  Example: -B851 .P49 2004-

Library Databases

College and university libraries increasingly rely on databases to provide digital versions of articles published in journals, magazines, newspapers, as well as other publications and materials. Generally, the databases are available to students and faculty through the Internet via the library home page, though a library card and a password may be required for off-campus access.

Library databases make use of online forms similar to that of a library computerized catalog. Searches are by subject, title, author, and name of publication. Advanced search features are available. Some databases provide full text of articles published in newspapers, journals, and magazines. Others give publication information only, such as title, author, publication, date of publication, and an abstract of the article. Popular databases include Lexis-Nexis Academic Universe, Academic Search Premier, and JSTOR.

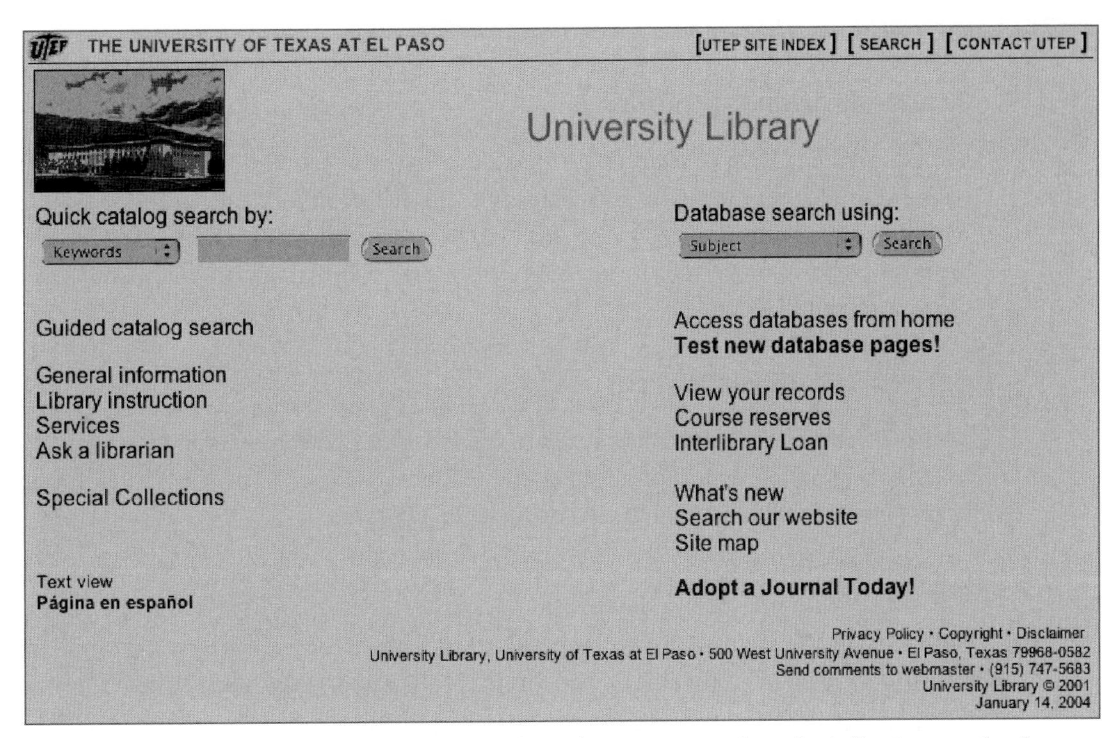

This university library Web site affords quick access to the computerized catalog, allowing searches by keywords, subject, author, title, and call number.

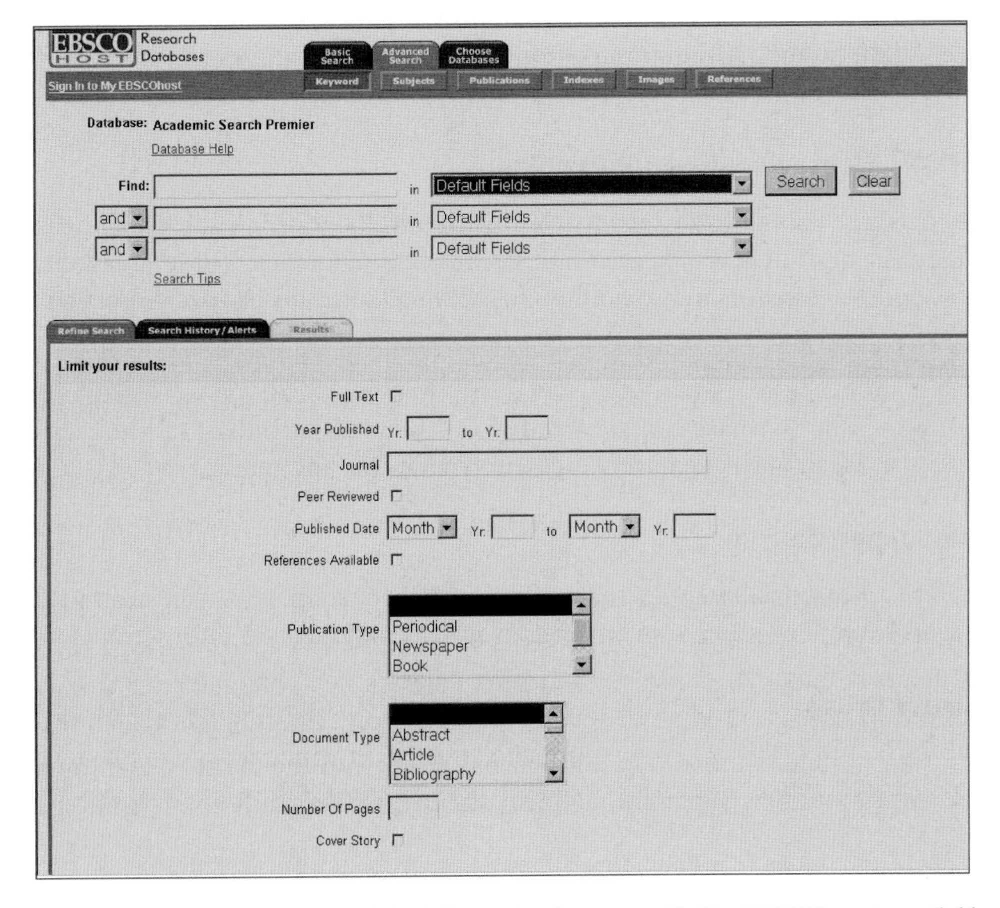

Academic Search Premier, one of the full-text databases provided by EBSCOhost, is available at many colleges and universities

Frequently Listed Databases

Academic Search Premier

This is an EBSCOhost database that contains full-text articles for almost 4000 academic, social sciences, humanities, general science, education and multi-cultural journals, many of which are peer-reviewed. It also offers abstracts of thousands more journals. This site contains full-text articles from a number of major print magazines and newspapers (full-text coverage from 1965 to present).

ArticleFirst (FirstSearch)

This is a searchable index of articles taken from the contents pages of nearly 12,500 journals in science, technology, medicine, social science, business, the humanities, and popular culture (full-text of selected articles from 1990-present).

InfoTrac Newspapers

This site provides access to full-text articles from over a hundred regional newspapers, including the Austin American-Statesman, Dallas Morning News, and Houston Chronicle.

Ingenta

Formerly known as Uncover, this database provides citations from 1988 to the present to articles from the tables of contents of approximately 25,000 journals and magazines that cover all disciplines. If the subscription of the university allows, you can purchase full-text articles. It can also be searched directly at http://www.gateway.ingenta.com.

JSTOR: Electronic Journal Archive

This database contains full-text articles from over 300 journals for fields including anthropology, Asian studies, ecology, economics, education, finance, history, mathematics, philosophy, political science, and sociology. Search in all journals or specify particular journals.

LexisNexis Academic

This LexisNexis database contains some 5,000 journals including full-text coverage of topics such as legal, business, government, current news, and medicine.

Newspaper Source

An EBSCOHost database, Newspaper Source offers current news from around the world with updates from newspaper wire services, as well as national and international newspapers.

Project Muse

This database offers more than 200 journal titles from the fields of literature, history, the arts, cultural studies, education, political science, gender studies, economics, and others.

PsycInfo

This is an EBSCOhost bibliographic index that provides citations, abstracts, and some full text for the field of psychology taken from journal articles, book chapters, books, dissertations, and technical reports. The coverage includes the psychological aspects of related disciplines.

Readers' Guide Abstracts

This is a FirstSearch database that corresponds to the printed Readers' Guide to Periodical-Literature. It contains selected full-text articles from magazines on a wide variety of topics including news, arts, education, business, sports, health, consumer affairs, and others.

Worldcat

This is a FirstSearch database that provides access to library catalogs from around the world. The database contains bibliographic records describing books, journals, maps, musical scores, manuscripts, etc.

The First-Year Writing Program Plagiarism Statement

The following statement defines and describes plagiarism, gives general guidelines and examples for using sources in essays, and sets the policies on plagiarism for courses in the First-Year Writing Program. Although policies on plagiarism may vary among courses and definitions of plagiarism may be extended in some fields, this statement offers guidelines and policies on plagiarism that are generally accepted in universities and colleges. Students in First-Year Writing Program courses will be asked to read and discuss this statement and sign a statement confirming that they understand it.

Plagiarism Defined

Plagiarism is claiming someone else's work as your own. Ideas circulate freely in an intellectual community, and intellectual inquiry often depends on use of ideas borrowed from others. Responsible writers, however, indicate their debts to others by clearly citing borrowed material. Plagiarism occurs when writers fail to cite their borrowings. Auto-plagiarism consists in plagiarizing yourself. In the context of your coursework as a student, auto-plagiarism would occur if you resubmitted any of your own work—whether a complete assignment or only part of it—as if it were freshly submitted.

Plagiarized work is easy to recognize because it does not clearly indicate borrowing. It is full of facts, observations, and ideas the writer could not have developed on his or her own and is written in a style different from that of the writer. By clearly indicating your debts to other writers, you can both avoid plagiarism and call attention to your own original ideas.

Integrating Sources

Understanding the different ways you can incorporate source material into your writing is crucial to avoiding plagiarism:

Quotation ("quote" for short): a word-for-word copy of someone else's words. Indicate a quoted passage by enclosing it in quotation marks ("") or, if it is longer than four lines, by setting it apart from the main text in an indented block. The source of the quotation must also be cited, either in the text or in a footnote or endnote.

Paraphrase: a restatement in your own words of something your source has said. One purpose of paraphrasing, as opposed to quoting, is to put something into words your audience will understand. For example, articles in popular science magazines often paraphrase more difficult articles in science journals. Putting something into your own words is an important intellectual activity in its own right: it shows that you understand and can work with the material. Putting an idea in your own words does not make it yours. Although neither quotation marks nor block indention are needed, a paraphrase must be cited.

Summary: resembles a paraphrase but is much shorter and follows the sources less closely than a paraphrase does. You must cite the source that you are summarizing.

Citation: identifies the source of a quotation, paraphrase or summary. Citation practices vary considerably in different types of writing, but most academic and professional writing requires a full citation in the text, in a combination of brief parenthetical citations in the text and complete bibliographic entries in a list of Works Cited, or in footnotes or endnotes.

Types of Plagiarism

1. **Direct Plagiarism:** This is copying a source word for word without indicating that it is a quotation and crediting the author.
2. **Borrowing Work from Other Students:** There is nothing wrong with students helping each other or sharing information, but you must write your own essays. This includes having another student dictate to you as you write their words down. Turning in a paper that someone else has written is an especially severe case of direct plagiarism.
3. **Vague or Incorrect Citation:** A writer should clearly indicate where borrowing begins and ends because not to do so, though it seems innocent, is plagiarism. ***This is why it is so important to learn a citation style such as MLA style*** (see next section for more information). Sometimes, a writer cites a source once, and the reader assumes that the previous sentence or paragraph has been paraphrased, when most of the essay is a paraphrase of this one source. The writer has failed to indicate his borrowings clearly. Paraphrases and summaries should be indicated as such by surrounding them with citation-—at the beginning with the author's name, at the end with a parenthetical reference. The writer must always clearly indicate when a paraphrase, summary, or quotation begins, ends, or is interrupted.
4. **Auto-Plagiarism:** This happens when an author plagiarizes his or her own writing. Students' best work usually occurs through revisions of previous drafts. But auto-plagiarism takes place when a student presents any prior writing, usually from another course or school, as entirely fresh work for course credit. A previous assignment—whether in whole or part—may **not** be offered as if it were a fresh submission to a course instructor.
5. **Mosaic Plagiarism:** This is the most common type of plagiarism. The writer does not copy the source directly, but changes a few words in each sentence or slightly reworks a paragraph, without giving credit to the original author. Those sentences or paragraphs are not quotations, but they are so close to quotation that they should be quoted directly or, if they have been changed enough to qualify as a paraphrase, the source should be cited.

Penalties for Plagiarism

No plagiarized paper will be accepted for credit in any First-Year Writing Program course at Texas A&M University-Corpus Christi. This includes partially plagiarized papers. A plagiarized paper will automatically receive an "F" grade. If the instructor feels that the plagiarism was unintentional, he or she may ask the student to rewrite the paper for credit. By reading this plagiarism handout and by affirming that you understand plagiarism, however, you assume responsibility for any plagiarism that occurs in your essays.

Plagiarism may be grounds for failure in a course. Even if a student's course grades average out to a passing grade when the "F" from a plagiarized paper is counted in, the instructor may still give the student an "F" for the course.

Instructors who suspect that a student has plagiarized will submit a letter explaining the reasons for their suspicions and a copy of the student's paper to the Coordinator of the FYWP, who will keep them on file. All cases of suspected plagiarism that occur in FYWP courses will be reviewed by the Coordinator. Any student who is suspected of plagiarism will have the opportunity to discuss the matter with the Coordinator of the FYWP.

Repeat offenders may be dismissed from the University, per the Student Code of Conduct.

Why Students Plagiarize

Some students are tempted to paraphrase because they find writing college-level essays difficult or intimidating. Such students sometimes become frustrated when an essay on which they have worked long and hard is returned with many corrections and a low grade. Frustrated and afraid of failure, they may resort to copying an essay word for word or making only a few slight changes in the wording.

Rather than plagiarizing, these students should seek assistance from their instructor, from the Writing Center, from the Tutoring and Learning Center, from the Disabilities Services Office, or from the Counseling Center, which can provide assistance in dealing with frustration, fear, and stress.

Other students write well enough but find plagiarism tempting because they fear earning a grade lower than they or their parents expect, have fallen behind in their coursework and feel that they lack the time to write a competent essay, or feel that they cannot handle the assigned task or generate good ideas on the subject.

Start writing, even if the writing begins as a summary of some other piece of writing, and you will usually discover that you have something to say. If you fall behind, talk with your instructor. He or she may penalize you for submitting work late, but late work is preferable to plagiarized work. If you feel overwhelmed by your course work and unable to keep up, arrange to visit a counselor at the Counseling Center. He or she can help you learn to manage your time and the stress of university life better.

Plagiarizing an essay is never an acceptable solution.

A Case of Plagiarism

Richard Marius, in his statement on plagiarism for Harvard University, cites a case of mosaic plagiarism. G. R. V. Barratt, in the introduction to ***The Decembrist Memoirs***, plagiarized from several works, including ***The Decembrists*** by Marc Raeff. In one passage, Raeff had written:

> December 14, 1825, was the day set for taking the oath of allegiance to the new Emperor, Nicholas I. Only a few days earlier, on November 27, when news of the death of Alexander I had reached the capital, an oath of allegiance had been taken to Nicholas's older brother, Grand Duke Constantine, Viceroy of Poland. But in accordance with the act of renunciation he had made in 1819, Constantine had refused the crown. The virtual interregnum stirred society and produced uneasiness among the troops, and the government was apprehensive of disorders and disturbances. Police agents reported the existence of secret societies and rumors of a coup to be staged by regiments of the Guards. The new Emperor was anxious to have the oath taken as quickly and quietly as possible. The members of the central government institutions—Council of

> State, Senate, Ministries—took the oath without incident, early in the morning. In most regiments of the garrison the oath was also taken peaceably.

Barratt presented the same paragraph with only a few words and details changed:

> December 14, 1825, was the day on which the Guards' regiments in Petersburg were to swear solemn allegiance to Nicholas I, the new Emperor. Less than three weeks before, when news of the death of Alexander I had reached the capital from Taganrog on the sea of Azov, an oath, no less solemn and binding, had been taken to Nicholas's elder brother, the Grand Duke Constantine, viceroy of Poland. Constantine, however, had declined to be emperor, in accordance with two separate acts of renunciation made in 1819 and, secretly, in 1822. The effective interregnum caused uneasiness both in society and in the army. The government feared undefined disorders—with some reason, since police agents reported the existence of various clandestine groups and rumours of a coup to be effected by guardsmen. Nicholas was anxious that the oath be sworn to him promptly and quietly. At first it would seem that he would have his way; senators, ministers, and members of the Council of State took the oath by 9 A. M. In most regiments of the garrison the oath was also taken peaceably.

To see why this is mosaic plagiarism, compare these two versions line by line. What changes has Barratt made? Why do you think he made these changes? Why is this a case of plagiarism even though Barratt has made changes?

Guidelines for Proper Use of Sources

1. Enclose direct quotations in quotation marks. If the quotation is longer than four lines, indent it in block format. In both cases, cite the source by using MLA in-text parenthetical style and by entering the source in the Works Cited page.
2. Use in-text parenthetical citation to cite paraphrases or summaries. Any key phrases that you borrow word-for-word should go in quotation marks.
3. Cite opinions, interpretations, and results of original research.
4. In general, do not cite statements of widely accepted fact; but when following a source closely, cite it even if the material is widely accepted fact. If you are unsure if something is a "widely accepted fact," then you should probably cite it. See your instructor if you have any questions about facts.

Ways To Avoid Plagiarism

1. When in doubt, CITE! It can never hurt to over-cite or cite when you don't need to.
2. Give yourself plenty of time to research and write your essay, so that you do not feel pressured because a topic proves unworkable at the last minute. When writing a paper that uses sources, give yourself time to digest the research and synthesize your findings.
3. Take careful research notes that include full bibliographic citations. If you forget to write down the bibliographic data, you may be tempted not to bother with the citation.
4. Make it a habit to put parenthetical citations for all the sources you borrow from in each draft you write.
5. Keep a good documentation guide handy or use an online resource when you are doing your research and writing your paper.
6. Have confidence in yourself. Even the best writers are often unaware of their good ideas and think they have nothing to say when their writing says a lot. Original ideas come from working closely with the ideas of others, not from flashes of inspiration.
7. Know where to get help. Start with your instructor and ask questions about citations about which you are not sure. Besides your instructor, you can consult a tutor in the

Writing Center for help with your writing. The reference librarians at Bell Library can help you with your research. The counselors at the Counseling Center can help you with problems like time management and stress. Students with learning disabilities should seek help from the Disabilities Services Office. Their services are confidential and free of charge. Finally, your academic advisor can help you put your course work in perspective, or help you make strategic decisions regarding your grades.

Conclusion

Learning how to use sources is one of the most important things you will learn in college. By using sources well and by clearly indicating your debts to these sources, your writing gains authority, clarity, and precision. Writers who plagiarize lose the advantages of belonging to an intellectual discourse community. If plagiarizers are professionals, they may be barred from practicing their profession, or their work may not be taken seriously. If they are students, they will carry the stigma of having plagiarized. Instructors will be suspicious of their work and will be unwilling to support any of their future efforts, write recommendations for them, or even work with them at all. Plagiarism is one of the worst mistakes anyone can make. The best way to avoid it is to be scrupulous about indicating quotation, paraphrase, and summary.

TEXAS A&M UNIVERSITY-CORPUS CHRISTI FIRST-YEAR WRITING PROGRAM PLAGIARISM STATEMENT ACKNOWLEDGEMENT FORM

This acknowledgement provides confirmation that the Plagiarism Statement has been read, discussed, and understood by all students in English 1301 and 1302.

Student Name and Banner ID Number: ______________________________

Course Name and Number: ______________________________

Section Number: ______________ **Semester and Year:** ______________

Instructor: ______________________________ **Time:** __________

____

(Please Print) last name first name

To Students: By signing this form, you confirm that you understand what plagiarism is, that you know the policies that pertain to plagiarism, and that you accept responsibility for any plagiarism in your work.

To Instructors: All students in your section [s] should read the entire plagiarism policy of the First-Year Writing Program and sign this form **at least one time** during their writing course work at Texas A&M University-Corpus Christi. For students who have already read the statement in a previous class, you should reiterate the highlights of the statement and ask them to sign the form as a reminder of their responsibility to adhere to the policy.

Date Plagiarism Statement was discussed: ______________________________

Instructor's Signature: ______________________________

Student's Signature: ______________________________ **Date:** ______________

CHAPTER 9

Portfolios (Glenn Blalock)

Your seminar leader and your composition teacher will use portfolio assessment as one of the primary ways to evaluate your performance in the seminar and in the composition course.

- You will earn a large percent of your seminar grade by assembling portfolios during the semester (see your specific seminar syllabus for details about schedule and the value of individual portfolios).
- The portfolios will be worth more in your composition course (see your specific composition course syllabus for details about schedule and the value of individual portfolios).
- Each time that a portfolio is due, you will submit only one portfolio that will be evaluated by your seminar leader and your composition teacher.

Follow the links below for the general instructions you will use to assemble your portfolios and for further explanation about portfolios--what they are and why we will use them. In addition to the information below, your seminar leader and composition teacher will address questions you have and may provide you with more specific instructions to ensure that your portfolio is relevant to your specific learning community.

What is a "Portfolio"?

We define a portfolio as a collection of work purposefully selected and intentionally assembled by a learner. The one piece of work that is required in all portfolios is an extensive reflective overview, a piece of writing that presents the portfolio contents to readers / evaluators and that explains why particular contents were chosen and what they are meant to show.

In our first-year composition classes and in the seminar, we encourage you to assemble your portfolio electronically, making your work available on the web. However, you can also submit your portfolio as a folder, with your work included.

The portfolio is not an assignment. Instead, it is the way we evaluate your work on all the assignments and activities that you have engaged in during the portfolio period. The only piece of writing that you will do exclusively for the portfolio is the reflective overview. It is, in a sense, your argument for a particular grade on that portfolio.

An effective portfolio will most likely not include "everything" you do during that part of the course. One of the principles of portfolio assessment is that the learner takes an active role in choosing work to include. In other words, you are responsible for selecting evidence that you think best demonstrates your performance, your learning, your development of specific skills and knowledge; you are responsible for helping portfolio readers understand your choices.

For many students, portfolios are problematic. Teachers will not prescribe "the" way to assemble a portfolio. Teachers will not provide a checklist of materials to include. Students have no one formula to follow, nor can they wait until the night before it is due to assemble and complete a portfolio that will earn a satisfactory grade. In other words, for many students, the portfolio prevents them from using the same methods in college that they used to succeed in high school. The portfolio process requires you to be an active learner, to value deep learning, to engage in the kinds of intellectual work that you haven't been asked to do before now. Portfolios require you to understand and practice critical thinking and information literacy skills.

You and your classmates will be frustrated at first when you face a portfolio assignment. Your teacher will not tell you precisely how to assemble it or what to include. Instead, teachers will ask you questions and challenge you to make choices about your portfolio based on your analysis of the audience and purpose (and the instructions provided). Your instructors will provide you with evaluation guidelines that you will use as you work on your portfolio, and they will invite you to help them write those guidelines. But you may be frustrated by those, too, because they will not describe only one way to earn a grade.

Recognize that your teachers are trying to introduce you to an advanced form of active learning, one that challenges you to take responsibility for your success. Your teachers will offer you more help than you want, but only after you have taken charge of the assignment. So share work in progress with your teachers and colleagues, ask them specific questions about the choices you have made, about the work you are doing.

Why Portfolios?

We use portfolio assessment in the First-Year Program because we think it is the most effective way to evaluate the fullest range of work you do. In addition, with the portfolio process, you have considerable responsibility (and independence) in helping determine how your performance will be evaluated. Your choice of evidence helps with our evaluation, and your reflective overview (a central part of the portfolio) helps your teachers understand what you include as evidence and why you include it. In other words, the portfolio gives teachers a broader and deeper view of student performance and learning than is possible with single tests or with single pieces of writing. Also, the portfolio process supports the First-Year Program's emphasis on metacognition, on "learning how to learn," and on learners being responsible for their own success. Your seminar leader and composition teacher will be discussing portfolios more fully during the semester. Be sure that you ask questions if you are unclear about how we will use portfolios.

Why Three?

Learning improves dramatically when learners receive timely feedback on their performances. Three portfolios offer teachers the opportunity to evaluate student performances regularly throughout the semester. In addition, the feedback on these portfolios will help students understand their status in the course from the very first weeks.

It is important to remember that these portfolios are sequential—they build on each other to lead students toward a deeper understanding and more complex manipulation of the critical thinking and information literacy concepts and tools that students will need to become successful, productive citizens and adults.

General Portfolio Instructions for Seminar and Composition:

For your portfolio, choose from among the various kinds of work you have done in your learning community courses or other courses in which you are enrolled to show evidence of:

- Developing and using your strengths to achieve success as a learner, as an individual in transition to the college environment, and as an informed and active citizen
  - For instance, in your course work (active learning, writing, reading, speaking, planning, listening, note taking, studying, problem-solving, time management) and in your relationships as a university student (conflict resolution, meeting and interacting with others, participating in student-sponsored activities, engaging in community service activities)
- Making connections among the courses in your learning community (and among all of the courses you are taking)
- Developing and using critical thinking skills
- Developing and using information literacy skills
- Developing and using skills for discussion as a way of learning
  - Active participation in class discussions (face to face or online)
- Developing and using skills for writing to learn
- Learning how to learn and taking responsibility for your success

Instructions that will be related directly to your composition course:

Include the Project Document

Show evidence of

- inquiry (critical thinking / information literacy)
- invention, drafting, revising, editing
  - planning, discussions with peers (online and f2f), multiple drafts
  - discussing revision strategies with writing consultant at Writing Center
- sharing and responding to work in progress
  - discussing revision strategies with writing consultant at Writing Center
  - may include a student instructor conference
- reflecting on process and learning experience

Each Portfolio will include an extensive, well-developed reflective overview

In an extensive, well developed reflective overview—one of the most important pieces of writing in your portfolio—explain to your teachers what you include, why you chose to include what you did, what those materials represent and how, specifically. This will be more than a mere description of contents. Instead, you will help readers understand how materials you have chosen are evidence of the kinds of learning / participation that you say they are. Include a section in your reflective overview that serves as self-assessment for the portfolio period. Based on the expectations for the portfolio, what grade do you think it should earn, and why.

This reflective overview will be the result of multiple drafts and peer review. It will represent careful, college level writing. It is more than a description. It is also an analysis and an evaluation of the materials. One way to think of the purpose of your overview is to persuade readers that your performance for the period of the portfolio should be evaluated in a certain way, earning a certain grade, with ample reasons to support your claims. Obviously, with this much to accomplish, the overview is important. Effective overviews will be several pages long, well organized, clear.

CHAPTER 10

Campus Writing Resources

Faculty

Faculty who teach first year classes, especially those who teach composition, but also those in other disciplines, should be your first stop for help with writing. Faculty all post office hours: time that they have committed to be in their offices to help students. If you have questions regarding assignments, grades, expectations for the course, readings, technology, or even something unrelated to your class, use these times to sit down with your instructors one-on-one to discuss these questions. The earlier you visit with faculty, the better they will be able to help you.

Faculty know best the expectations for their assignments, so speaking with them directly should be the first action you take when you are confused. Be sure, however, to have read the assignment before asking questions. Faculty do not want to explain verbally what they have already explained in an assignment description or on their website.

In addition to face-to-face contact, most faculty use email extensively and will respond to student questions by email. When approaching faculty virtually, be sure to address them politely, ask your questions clearly, and sign your email with your name and even the section or course you are enrolled in. Some faculty have hundreds of students and may not otherwise know who you are, or what assignment you're referring to.

Writing Center/TLC

The Writing Center at Texas A&M University-Corpus Christi helps students, from incoming first year students to doctoral candidates, improve their writing. Writing Center consultants work one-on-one with writers at all stages of the writing process to help them find ideas, organize their thoughts, cite sources, and prepare assignments for classes and documents such as application letters and resumes. We strive to provide an active, constructive audience for any writing task. The Writing Center collaborates with the First-Year Program to ensure that all first-year students have a common vocabulary and experience with the demands and expectations of college level writing.

Location: Bell Library 216

Writing Center URL: http://critical.tamucc.edu/wiki/WC/Home/

General Services

The Writing Center offers assistance with a variety of writing projects - in all disciplines:

- Research and scientific papers
- Reflective writing
- Presentation planning and review
- Collaborative writing
- Scholarship and graduate school application essays

Assistance with all stages in the writing process:

- Topic selection
- Brainstorming and pre-writing – getting started
- Framing research questions and locating resources
- Organization
- Draft Review – multiple drafts encouraged
- Document formatting and citations- according to MLA, APA and other recognized styles

ELL and International Students

For students who are English Language Learners, the Writing Center offers all of the above, plus:

- Special attention to the standard use of articles: "the," "a," and "an"
- Assistance with grammar and idiomatic phrasing
- Longer sessions available
- Frequent sessions encouraged

THEA-liable (ENGL 0099)

Students who have not passed the Writing portion of the THEA or alternative assessment must meet with the Writing Consultants for 30 minutes once a week for the entire semester as part of the contract they will sign with the Intervention Specialists. Go to library room 216-D to make arrangements.

Bell Library

Located in the center of campus, Bell Library provides writers with reliable, scholarly sources for research. Reference Librarians are available to assist in the use of the databases, which list thousands of articles in a range of disciplines, as well as legal and government documents and newspaper and media publications. In addition to virtual resources, Bell Library holds a sizable periodical and book collection, media services, course reserves, as well as many places for students to study: couches, tables, desks, and group rooms. Hours and databases are available online:

Bell Library URL: http://rattler.tamucc.edu/

Campus Computer Labs, Laptop Permission, and Islander Email

Open computer labs are available all around campus; additionally, students can access the wireless network if they obtain permission. All students need to use their Islander email accounts. Vital information regarding issues such as registration, financial aid, holds, and correspondence from faculty and any campus emergency alert information will occur through this account.

Directions for setting up permission for wireless device use and for accessing your email account and setting it up to forward to any address you wish are available on the Microcomputer Lab website.

Microcomputer Lab URL: http://labs.tamucc.edu/

Sand Paper (printing)

Students can print in an open computer lab if they have funds deposited on their SandDollar card.

Wiki Basics

Introduction

Wiki (taken from the Hawaiian wiki-wiki meaning fast-fast) is a web-editing tool that allows for collaborative creation and editing of websites by using a simple mark-up language. Most of your instructors in seminar and composition use wiki sites for course information and the university provides all students wiki spaces for both academic and personal use. The TAMU-CC wiki sites are password protected for editing off campus and uploading files. Seminar or composition instructors will provide those passwords in class.

Basic Commands

Wiki is designed to be a self-taught program language. The version of wiki used at TAMU-CC (PmWiki) has instructions on basic commands at the bottom of each page in the *edit* view.

There are two basic commands that are needed for using wiki in coursework: creating a new page and attaching a file.

- To create a new page, type [[page name]] in the edit view. When saved, the page will now how a link which looks like: page name
- To attach a file, type [[Attach:filename.ext*|Document Name]] in the edit view. When saved, the page will now have a place to upload a file, and will look like: Document Name.
  - From here, click on Document Name, fill in password, and then attach (upload) a file in the same way a file would be attached a to an email or MySpace page.
  - *Must match the file extension:.doc, .ppt, .ext, .rtf

For more help an instructional program located on at:

http://firstyear.tamucc.edu/wiki/Main/HomePage, For Students, Wiki Self Help PowerPoint.

WebCT Basics

Introduction

Unlike wiki, WebCT is a closed website which some composition or large lecture instructors will use. Instructors use WebCT to deliver course contents such as syllabi, assignments, facilitate discussions, deliver instructional materials, and grades. Instructors have the ability to hide or publish material to individual students, which insures that no unauthorized person views sensitive materials such as grades.

Logging on to WebCT

WebCT is accessible from the main TAMU-CC web page at: http://www.tamucc.edu.

- Click on the link located on the right-hand navigation entitled The Island Online.
- First time login, click on Login Help to obtain WebCT ID and password
- Click on Login to WebCT
- Complete WebCT ID and password

Scanning/scanner help at TLC

In conjunction with wiki use, instructors may require submission of projects such as portfolios online. Students, therefore, must become proficient in the use of scanners. The Tutoring and Learning Center (TLC) and the Media Center in Bell Library have flatbed scanners available for student use. Both are located on the second floor of the library, and the TLC has student workers available to assist students in scanner use.

Citation generators available for free online

Introduction

Citation generators are tools that generate reference citations using a drop-down fill-in-the blank templates and will generate citations in the most common styles such as APA, Chicago, and MLA. Most are citation generators are free, however, some may require a small usage fee, or are a combination of free and fee. Depending on the site, users may be able to download their citations as a MS WORD© document, or users may be required to copy, paste, and then reformat the citation into a MS WORD© document.

Citation Generators

Below are three of the most popular citation generators available:

- Son of Citation Machine http://citationmachine.net/index.php?new_style=x#here
  - Provides APA, Chicago, and MLA. Copy and paste into WORD© file; provides parenthetical citation information.
- Knight Cite Citation Generator http://www.calvin.edu/library/knightcite/
  - Provides APA, Chicago, and MLA. Requires a free registration and after registration will save work as WORD© file to download.
- Noodletools Citation Generator Bib Express http://www.noodletools.com
  - Provides APA and MLA. Free copy and paste into WORD© file; has for-fee services available also.

Using Technology

Courses in the FYLCP often require the use of other technology in addition to wiki and WebCT. Formal academic papers are word-processed and students are often asked to use programs such as MS PowerPoint© or MS Excel© for routine course assignments. Using technology is not at the whim of individual instructors, but is a learning objective of the University Core Curriculum Program to make students better able to be engaged citizens of the 21st century. As such, individual instructors are required to incorporate technology in their day-to-day class plans. However, the program realizes that some students may need support in using technology so there are various ways to get technology help on campus, such as the Micro Computer Lab at the TLC.

Some points to remember about technology on the TAMU-CC campus:

- As of summer 2008 the computers at the university do not have MS Office© 2007. Students who have new computers with MS Office© 2007 must back save all files as an earlier file version to be able to open files on campus computers.
- Campus computers will not open word-processing programs such as Corel® WordPerfect® or Microsoft Works®. Students who have these programs on their computers can obtain a free word-processing program from OpenOffice.org at http://www.openoffice.org/. This is an organization dedicated to promoting free share-ware software. The Office-like download will provide Microsoft compatible word-processor, spreadsheet, database, and presentation programs. The word-processing program is not exactly like MS WORD®, but it is compatible, so users will be able to open files on campus computers.
- An anti-virus program is another necessity for students using their personal computers. A computer virus can disable a computer and most instructors will view having a computer virus as a "dog ate my homework" excuse. Students who do not have an anti-virus program on their computer can download a free program from Gristsoft at: http://free.grisoft.com/ww.download?prd=afe.

Disability Services

Students with permanent or temporary disabilities who qualify for support under Section 504 of the Rehabilitation Act and the Americans with Disabilities Act of 1990 must self-identify and register with the Director of the Disability Services (DS). To qualify for services, students must 1) be admitted to the University, 2) present appropriate and current documentation of their disability from a qualified professional and 3) register with the DS Office each semester. Advance planning by the student with the Director or Assistant Director of the DS Office is necessary to ensure adequate time to arrange for appropriate accommodations. It is recommended that requests for services and/or academic adjustments be made as soon as possible. Requests for services requiring extensive preparation (e.g., interpreter services, adaptive and assistive equipment, textbooks in alternate format, etc.), may need up to 30 days to process. For additional information, please call (361) 825-5816 or visit the DS website at http://disabilityservices.tamucc.edu

Disability Services Office: Driftwood 101, 825-5816

Additional Campus Resources, Rules, and Information

The *Islander Student Planner* has further information on campus resources, a full copy of the Student Code of Conduct, and many other helpful tips. The planner is provided FREE to students. It is distributed first come, first served, at *Passport to the Island*, planned for September 2nd, 4-7 pm, in the library breezeway. Copies will be available at Wells Fargo, the Round Building, and the UC Information Desk after September 2.

[Talk-2-Me] is a phone number you can call to be directed to other resources and/or have questions answered.

CHAPTER 11

Sample Student Writing

Orion Powell
Dr. Susan Murphy
ENG.1301: Composition I
26 October 2007

ANNOTATED BIBLIOGRAPHY

Baldrica, Diana. "FUEL economy; Typically, gas prices fall after Labor Day. Not this year." McClatchy Newspapers, Inc. [Fresno Bee] 16 Sept. 2007, final ed.: Pg. F1. Lexis-Nexis. Lexis-Nexis. Mary & Jeff Bell Library. 29 Sept. 2001 <http://0-www6.lexisnexis.com>.

According to this article, the price of gas usually goes down after every summer, but it will more than likely not happen this time. This article supports the idea that the rise of gas prices has a negative impact on society and the continuous high price of gasoline does not help people in any way. While other things may get cheaper, the cost of gasoline will not. It's been shown throughout the nation that the price at gas pumps are increasing. The price of gas usually goes down after Labor day because less people are going out on vacations. In September, a few days hit a record on the price of crude oil.

Carroll, Jim. "Gas prices up again." *Erie Times-News* [Pennsylvania] 21 Sept. 2007: 1+. *Lexis-Nexis.* Lexis-Nexis. Mary & Jeff Bell Library. 25 Sept. 2007 <http://0-www6.lexisnexis.com>.

This article talks about a man named Earl Long who owns a F-250 pickup and a trailer. He makes constant trips from Greensburg to Erie and back which costs him about $150 in gas. He traded in his previous diesel powered truck for the F-250 pickup. This was suppose to be a way to save more money from fuel costs. According to the Federal energy analysts, "crude oil supplies in the U.S. are low, and demand for gasoline and diesel fuel remain strong." This helps give the idea of why oil companies may want to raise their prices on diesel and gasoline altogether. Overseas competition for crude oil isn't helping lower the price of our everyday fuel. This article also introduces the idea of how you have to spend more in gasoline resulting in you having to end up spending less in other things. This articles relates to my work because as prices of gasoline increase it impacts the general population as well as college students.

Curtis, Susan, and Najah Shani. "The Effect of Taking Paid Employment During Term-time on Students' Academic Studies." *Journal of Further & Higher Education* 26.2 (2002): p129-138. *EBSCOhost.* EBSCO. Mary & Jeff Bell Library. 15 Oct. 2007 <http://0-web.ebscohost.com.portal.tamucc.edu>.

This article talks about the affects of working while having to study for school classes. There is data shown supporting that more students are working in comparison to previous years. Because of having a job, students were more likely to have lower grades and even miss lectures. This article supports the idea that students have a job because they must pay for housing, living costs, school costs, and especially gasoline. As a result of having a job, there is a disadvantage to the student's grades. This relates to my work because it shows the disadvantage of having a job in order to pay for gasoline.

Dotson, Brett. Personal interview. 15 Oct. 2007.

In the interview I had with Brett, I asked him several questions about the effects gasoline prices are having on him as a college student. He told me that he has been going to TAMUCC for 5 years now, has a job, and lives nowhere near his job or school. He states that the more he pays in gas means that he has less to spend on food and recreational activities. He believes that the oil companies are taking advantage of the public. He would never let an outrageous gas price keep him from attending school. He thinks that his job could pay him more so that gasoline wouldn't seem as if it's costing so much. There are several places he would like to travel to but can not because of the price of gasoline. If he absolutely had to, he would use a means of public transportation or start a car pool. He would never consider walking to school because he lives too far from it. He believes that the price of gasoline effects him as a college student because students generally don't have a lot of money. This interview with Brett helps support my article because it relates to the issue of gasoline prices while he's currently a student.

Hitchcox, Alan L. "A silver lining to high gas prices." *Hydraulics & Pneumatics* 57.6 (2004): p.1-2. *EBSCOhost.* EBSCO. Mary & Jeff Bell Library. 25 Sept. 2007 <http://search.ebscohost.com>.

This article discusses the issues that several people are having with the price of gasoline. A lot of people appear to be complaining about the price of gas being over $2.00 which is about a 30% increase in what most people are used to. People who receive a lower income have a tougher time dealing with the issue of high gas prices. This is noted especially if they travel long distances to a job every other day. These people with lower incomes typically have to reduce the purchases they make on other things. For the past few decades the price of gasoline had been increasing at a slower rate compared to the cost of living, until now. This article helps support the idea that the rising cost of gasoline in comparison from several decades ago can lead to a disadvantage in the

Lyman, F. "Clean cars." *Technology Review* 93.4 (1990): p.22-22. *EBSCOhost.* EBSCO. Mary & Jeff Bell Library. 1 Oct. 2007 <http://0-web.ebscohost.com>.

This article talks primarily about alternative fuels and I use the topic of alternative fuels to suggest how they aren't very helpful because they always tag along some sort of disadvantage. The article discusses how petroleum is one of the mostly used fuels in cars and has been for the past century. Alternative fuels are made to help reduce pollutants and to make a switch to another type of fuel. An energy consultant named James Cannon in this article supports compressed natural gas. It is less harmful than gasoline and methanol and costs less expensive but it only lasts half as long as cars that run on petroleum. Methanol gives off a lot more horsepower and acceleration to a car but it has its disadvantages. It burns the skin and peels paint, an ounce could kill a man if he swallowed it, and cars have a hard time starting if the temperature is below 50 degrees Fahrenheit. Mixing the methanol with 15% gasoline and 85% methanol can help solve the problem so it can start at lower temperatures. Ethanol is less toxic and more powerful but it costs about twice as much as gasoline if made from corn. This article discusses a good issue in an attempt to try and find another fuel source other than gasoline although due to the many disadvantages these different fuels have it may be better to stick to gasoline. This relates to my article because even with the invention of a car that uses an alternative fuel, college students usually can not afford a new car considering that they are already having a hard time paying for the current gasoline to fuel their cars.

Pluviose, David. "Community Colleges and Their Students Breaking the Bank to Fill the Tank." *Community College Week* 26 Sept. 2005: p.3-14. *EBSCOhost.* EBSCO. Mary & Jeff Bell Library. 1 Oct. 2007 <http://0-web.ebscohost.com>.

This article gives information and data that discusses the noticeably risen price in comparison to previous years. For example, according to the U.S. Energy and Information Administration, "as of Sept. 5 the average price per gallon of regular gasoline in the U.S. was $3.06, up 65 percent from a year ago." This article also talks about how many SUV and big truck owners are trading in the vehicles for smaller vehicles and hybrids because of the high price of gasoline. This relates to my article because college students are affected directly because if they have a job, the little amount of money they make go into gasoline to get to school. Because most college students don't make much money they can't trade in their vehicles for more fuel efficient vehicles because they too cost a great deal of money. This article also talks about how most students can hardly pay for the gas to get them to school, they are generally stuck in a tough position of having to scrape up enough money to pay for the gasoline. This article helps support the idea of how the rise in gasoline prices is affecting college students.

Feature Story Assignment

Vision Statement Writing a feature story on an issue that impacts our society.

Task You are writing/creating/composing a feature story on a controversial social issue.

Purpose/Context To investigate a topic of your choice, possibly connected to your experience, your passions, your concerns. The context of this feature story is a news magazine or magazine for a popular audience.

Genre A feature story is an extended article written by a journalist or freelance writer, arising out of a need in society or current event that raises concerns and questions. The social issue must be something that different groups of people realistically view in very different ways; in other words, it must be controversial. It must be relevant to people in our society. The feature story must outline the key "facts" of the issue and the various perspectives, supported by the evidence cited by those groups. It might explore various "solutions" presented by various groups re: the topics. It is supported by research, including possibly interviews, and sources for facts in the article are attributed to in-text.

Source List In addition to the in-text attribution to sources, you will prepare an annotated bibliography of your sources in APA or MLA format.

Discourse Community The discourse community you are apprenticing to in this project is the journalism profession. Journalists who write feature stories are usually not personally invested in the issue, but response to a current event, press release, or other motivating factor to write their story. They usually write for money, but also seek to reveal the truth of an issue, and/or to improve people's lives by informing them of new information or more in-depth information.

Rhetorical Situation You are the author. Your audience are people interested in your issue who read the magazine/journal/newspaper that you identify as your target medium. You are informing them about the various perspectives on an issue, what controversies surround that issue, and possible solutions presented by various groups for the issue.

Orion Powell
Dr. Susan Murphy
ENG.1301: Composition I
26 October 2007

GAS PRICES AND THEIR HIDEOUS AFFECT ON COLLEGE STUDENTS

As an active college student without much money you can see yourself heading towards your college, to your work, then home, and then you may begin to notice the gasoline gauge on your car every time it gets near the "E" mark. Gasoline prices these days really aren't helping the sparse pocket change we have accumulated. As much as we may love driving our luxurious cars around town, having to fork over your diminishing pocket change for gasoline greatly discourages us.

http:// fotosearch.com

Most of us don't want to end up having to ride the city bus or walk to school because it seems troublesome and inconvenient. We also shouldn't have to ride the bus or walk to school if we are the owner of a vehicle. It defeats the purpose of owning a vehicle. But sometimes tough times call for difficult measures.

Sometimes when college students are out of money, there are only a few options that can be considered. We can pull some saved cash from our banking account that you may have from saving throughout the years. You can also begin asking for allowances from relatives or doing more work around the house to earn an allowance. Another option you can consider is to get a job or if you have one you can then work more hours. The only problem with working so much is that it can begin to affect your studying time, and thus your class grades.(Curis and Shani, 129) According to Alan Hitchcox, another suggestion is to "cut back on some other necessity (probably cigarettes or lottery tickets…)". Many people may also agree with the idea of having to give up other things in order to pay for gasoline. For example, according to Brett Dotson, "The more I have to pay for gas, the less I have to pay for food or recreational activities."

On September 5, 2007, "the average price per gallon of regular gasoline in the U.S. was $3.06, up 65 percent from a year ago."(Pluviose, 4) Every other year for the past few decades the price of gasoline has noticeably been augmenting gradually. This is showing that the cost of gasoline doesn't have any intention in decreasing any time soon.

http://mncorn.org

"The cost of crude oil, which is refined into gasoline and other petroleum products, increased 10% in the last month and hit a record Thursday [Sept. 11] at $80.09 a barrel."(Carroll, 1) When the cost of crude oil rises, it typically affects the price of gasoline. Usually the price of gasoline decreases at the end of the summer, but it is evident that it may not happen this year.(Baldrica, F1) When I asked Brett Dotson what he thought about the rising gas prices, he responded stating, "I think that the oil companies are taking advantage of the public. They like to play games shutting down refineries, raising the prices, later lowering it down a little, raise the prices again, and they do this until the public becomes accustom to their high prices."

Compressed natural gas, methanol, and ethanol are only a few alternative fuel sources that have been used in cars to try and find possibly better and cheaper fuel. Compressed natural gas may cost less, but "cars using it travel only half as far between refueling as those running on petroleum."(Lyman, 22) Methanol is "sometimes hard to start when the temperature falls below 50 degrees Fahrenheit…", and it "it burns the skin and peels paint."(Lyman, 22) According to Lyman, "one problem with ethanol is that it costs twice as much as gasoline." Alternative fuels are difficult to choose as a more reliable choice from one another because while some alternatives fuels may have an advantage to it, it may also have a far worst disadvantage.

Even with the option of alternative fuels, most students are "unable to afford hybrids or trade their cars in for more fuel efficient new models."(Hitchcox, 2)

Crystal Blackmon, a student at the Community College of Baltimore County in Catonsville. Md. stated, "I'm only working on work-study. You can't make enough to travel.... The work-study money isn't enough to pay for gas and to live."(Pluviose, 4) When you work for your school, you're only allowed to work so many hours and then the amount of money that you make is hardly sufficient to pay for gasoline, car insurance, and other living needs.

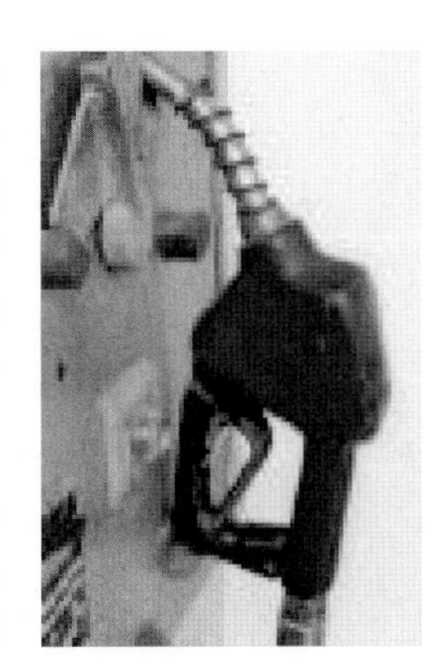

http:// slashfood.com

Despite the idea that the money you earn from work is hardly sufficient to pay for gas and to live, it might also be keeping you from traveling during your vacation time. "… there are many places that I would like to travel to such as the beach but I have to cartel those activities because of the price of gas."(Dotson)

There have been several different methods and ideas to attempting to resolve the problem of gas prices. Some methods and ideas that are going around are bus transportation, alternative fuels, cutting back on other costly things, and getting a job or working more hours. Although there are alternatives to having to pay so much for gasoline, these alternatives often carry a disadvantage. No one really wants to ride the bus when they own a vehicle, the cars that use these alternative fuels are quite expensive, working more can affect your grades, and cutting back on costly things such as food can leave you starving most of the time. As much as we want to avoid having to pay so much for gasoline, college students are going to continue having to deal with it for as long as they can.

WORKS CITED

Baldrica, Diana. "FUEL economy; Typically, gas prices fall after Labor Day. Not this year." *McClatchy Newspapers, Inc.* [Fresno Bee] 16 Sept. 2007, final ed.: Pg. F1. *Lexis-Nexis.* Lexis-Nexis. Mary & Jeff Bell Library. 29 Sept. 2001 <http://0-www6.lexisnexis.com>.

Carroll, Jim. "Gas prices up again." *Erie Times-News* [Pennsylvania] 21 Sept. 2007: 1+. *Lexis-Nexis.* Lexis-Nexis. Mary & Jeff Bell Library. 25 Sept. 2007 <http://0-www6.lexisnexis.com>.

Curtis, Susan, and Najah Shani. "The Effect of Taking Paid Employment During Term-time on Students' Academic Studies." *Journal of Further & Higher Education* 26.2 (2002): p129-138. *EBSCOhost.* EBSCO. Mary & Jeff Bell Library. 15 Oct. 2007 <http://0-web.ebscohost.com.portal.tamucc.edu>.

Dotson, Brett. Personal interview. 15 Oct. 2007.

Hitchcox, Alan L. "A silver lining to high gas prices." *Hydraulics & Pneumatics* 57.6 (2004): p.1-2. *EBSCOhost.* EBSCO. Mary & Jeff Bell Library. 25 Sept. 2007 <http://search.ebscohost.com>.

Lyman, F. "Clean cars." *Technology Review* 93.4 (1990): p.22-22. *EBSCOhost.* EBSCO. Mary & Jeff Bell Library. 1 Oct. 2007 <http://0-web.ebscohost.com>.

Pluviose, David. "Community Colleges and Their Students Breaking the Bank to Fill the Tank." *Community College Week* 26 Sept. 2005: p.3-14. *EBSCOhost.* EBSCO. Mary & Jeff Bell Library. 1 Oct. 2007 <http://0-web.ebscohost.com>.

Researched Argument Essay

Task You will produce at least two different, polished projects: one a formal, researched essay, and the other(s) visual, electronic, and/or multimedia arguments to act, which will be presented at the First Year Celebration.

Purpose/Context Based on your research in project two, you are now constructing an argument to persuade readers to take action re: your chosen topic. The context in which this occurs depends on your topic, but we suggest that you find a local focus if at all possible.

Genre Arguments are everywhere. Arguments that ask you to act include political advertisements, commercials, non-profit fund-raising letters, and even this assignment. For this assignment you will produce at least two different pieces, choosing different genres, different modes (fiction / non-fiction), or different media. Each piece will be addressing the same issue or problem, and each piece will be attempting to persuade readers to act.

Discourse Community Who argues? Everyone argues. We argue about different things and we have influence in different realms. Your discourse community will be determined by who is engaged in your topic.

Rhetorical Situation You can think of this assignment as an action plan, with examples of texts; as a campaign, with different kinds of texts; and/or as a multi media presentation. Your goal is to translate your academic work into writing that reaches a popular audience.

Research Essay

For Project Three you are charged with writing a formal, researched essay that presents several solutions to this issue/problem, while taking into account the concept of multiple perspectives leading to multiple solutions.

Considering the issue of solutions to this conflict / problem from three differing perspectives you will offer one solution--or combination of solutions--that you think is most likely to persuade people to act on the problem. Consider how the framing of the problem affects the possible solutions. Consider the consequences of the various solutions and consider how readers might choose among the possible solutions.

This project explains in detail at least the prevalent solutions you researched, considers how the framing of the problem affects the possible solutions, considers consequences of the various solutions and consider how readers might choose among the possible solutions. Think of this work as your proposal on how you will create writing that is meant to encourage / persuade readers to ACT, to join the ongoing conversation about the issue you have identified.

Tim Harlow
October 7, 2007
English 1301

THE CASE FOR UNIVERSAL HEALTH CARE

The United States typically prides itself on being the greatest nation in the world, yet is lagging behind when it comes to the health of its citizens. We consistently rank poorly in health statistics when compared to other developed countries, while spending more per person than any nation in the world. The main distinction from the health care of America to those of the world's leading nations in these statistics is our refusal to provide universal health coverage. By adopting a carefully planned universal health care system, the United States will be able to decrease health care costs, increase health care quality, and insure every citizen.

Most countries with universal health care can be divided into two categories based upon which system they use: single-payer and two tiered. Under a single-payer system, the government works as a huge not-for-profit insurance company, meaning that medical bills are simply sent to a federal or state department. Hospitals and doctor offices may or may not remain privately owned. This system is used in Denmark, Sweden, and Canada, but is also very similar to Medicare in the United States. Since a single-payer system is only defined by the nature of health-care financing, there is great variation among single-payer countries with some such as Britain owning every aspect of the nation's health-care, and others such as Canada, which has private hospitals and where physicians are not government employees. (AMSA) A two-tiered system allows for even more variation. In this program, an arrangement must be in place to guarantee public health care, but there are many different possibilities for parallel private systems to coexist alongside. (WHO)

Despite socialistic programs such as Medicare, Medicaid, and veterans' health care, the United States is not considered to be either of the previously mentioned systems because health is not guaranteed. As of 2005, 16% of Americans are un-insured and health care provided by employment is decreasing (NCHC). Also, according to the *CIA World Fact Book*, we have worse infant mortality than 40 other countries, are ranked 45th in overall life expectancy, and research from the *World Health Organization* ranks our health system as 37th when compared to other countries. Despite all of this we have the most expensive health care in the world, with average costs upwards of $5,711 per person, and taking up 15% of the total GDP (Kaiser). Meanwhile, the highest ranking health systems are consistently publicly funded and spend much less than we do per person, and as a percentage of GDP. In comparison, France, which has the highest ranked health-care in the world, spends $3,500 per capita and still manages to have more physicians and hospital beds per 1,000 people (WHO) (NationMaster). The combination of these many facts begins the argument for universal health care in the United States.

One of the major problems with our current system is simply that over 46 million people are left without any form of health insurance (Cbpp). While this situation in itself is unfortunate, the cost of these un-insured places a burden on the insured population. Over $100 billion per year is spent by the United States government to provided health care for uninsured patients (NCHC). These patients are dependent on emergency room care, and are 30 to 50 percent more likely to be kept in the hospital for preventable problems (NCHC).

After the patient is out of the hospital and unable to pay, the bill is subsidized through taxes. "Now, the cost of emergency care for the un-insured is built into hospital rates charged to insured patients, raising insurance by $1,000 each year" (Bouman).

Another argument that is often raised supporting the current system is that management by the private sector results in more efficiency, yet the statistics indicate that this is not the case. In the United States, health care corporations currently spend between 31 percent of premiums on administration and profits, while Canada's only spends 16.7 (PNHP). "*The Health Care Finance Administration calculates that the United States would save enough money administering our health care system though a single payer to provide health care for our 44 million uninsured, while avoiding managed care and allowing free choice of providers*" (Batista).

The inefficiency caused by corporate medicine also reduces the overall quality of healthcare. Over 41% of for-profit patients have been forced to change physicians, disrupting the continuity of their care (Committee). Increasingly, highly trained providers are being replaced, or their services "augmented" with less trained providers. Physicians are discouraged from advocating for their patients for fear of being "de-listed" by corporate providers, which may be part of the reason over 70% of physicians believe managed care negatively affects the overall quality of patient care (Committee).

Although, as shown, many of the arguments used against universal health care hold little water, there are very real issues which can arise from fully socializing medicine in a country. Britain, where almost every aspect of health care is government owned and operated, represents the most extreme form of socialization, making it a prime example to show the potential problems of taking away a private sector. Citizens of Britain are 21% more likely to die than Americans after being diagnosed with breast cancer, and are 38% more likely to die after being diagnosed with prostate cancer (Martin). This is accredited to cost cutting in the British health care system, where doctors are much less likely to prescribe medicine to prevent heart disease and there are fewer CT and MRI scanners per person (Reiland). Another aspect which could have led to this is the waiting times in the British system. According to the February 2005 issue of the British Magazine *The Spectator,* "In Britain, 36 percent of patients have to wait more than four months for non-emergency surgery. In the U.S., five percent do. In Britain, 40 percent of cancer patients do not see a cancer specialist." (Reiland) Although emergency surgery is done immediately, wait times for preventative surgery and medical check-ups can perpetuate a serious medical problem. Speeding up wait times has also become an important political issue in Canada, though Canadians do not possess the problems of overall quality which Britain has, and still retains a private sector (Health Canada). It is important to note that despite problems with the British and Canadian health systems, both countries are ranked higher than the United States by the World Health Organization, and have better life expectancies (CIA Fact Book).

The above facts illustrate the potential issues health care systems may face when delving too deeply into full socialization, though the two-tiered health care of France may represent the best of both worlds. Although much of health-care in France is privately administrated, those in the poorest percentile are completely reimbursed for medical payments, while reimbursed income decreases incrementally as patient income increases. The remainder is usually covered by private insurance, which is often provided by employment (Green). With the government covering most health care costs, more companies would be able to affordably insure their employees, and perhaps in America, we would see a reverse in the current trend of insurance provided by employment decreasing. Also, though many of the hospitals are private, public hospitals are introduced for the purpose of competing with the private sector, and in effect, maintains a consistent level of quality. Private hospitals can choose to qualify for patient reimbursement by meeting standards for pricing negotiated by the hospitals and the government, or simply operate within their own price range (Green). According to Victor G. Rodwin, professor of health policy and management at New York University, "The French approach suggests it is possible to solve the problem of financing universal coverage...[without] reorganizing the entire system," (Business Week). Other benefits are the opportunity to see a health-care physician as often as necessary, access to the highest quality technology, consumer choice, and little wait (Dutton) (Green).

Universal health care is often viewed as nothing more than a huge government bureaucracy dictating and rationing health care to the citizens, when in fact, there are many countries, such as the previous example, which retain a strong private sector. A true democracy should always be subject to the will of its people, meaning if problems with wait times, under-funding for research and medical equipment, or any other serious issues arise, there would be an accountable entity, rather than our current private system where companies are only accountable to their share holders. Even if the safety net of democratic choice failed in any of these areas, a great incentive would exist for private companies to meet the demands. The only way a health business could exist in such a system is if proves to exceed government standards. Ideally, a properly implemented two-tier nation would not only have market competition, but a democratically set standard to live up to.

Those in opposition to universal health care have a very interesting dilemma. Aside from the obvious argument of whether or not it is morally defensible for the richest nation on the plant to ignore the needs of its poorest citizens, a more straight forward argument exist: Is it rational to maintain business as usual when thirty-six countries surpass us in overall quality? Americans must ask themselves the reasons why their country compares so pitifully in health standards to the rest of the industrialized world. In two-tier nations such as France lies the hope that the United States can achieve the coverage and quality of European countries, while maintaining short waits and access to the best technology. Regardless of which specific alterations would be most effective, both sides agree the current condition of our health care is in drastic need of improvement. The role of the average citizen is important in the path towards universal health care, and will ultimately determine if a policy is to be implemented. Public dissatisfaction with our current system has already led to many presidential candidates placing a variety of health plans on their platforms, with a few hinting at universal coverage. Although the attainment of universal health care will require much more than a single presidential election, the possibility of achieving a sustainable health care system which benefits all Americans is certainly worth the effort.

Tim Harlow

WORKS CITED

AMSA Single Payer 101. Ed. Kao Ping. 5 Oct. 2007 <http://www.amsa.org/uhc/singlepayer101.pdf>.

Batista, John. "Corporate Medicine is Bad Medicine." The Voice [Winsted, CT] Dec. 1997

Bouman, John. "Everyone pays for the uninsured." Daily South Town 22 Mar. 2007. Shriver Center. 7 Oct. 2007 <http://www.povertylaw.org/news-and-events/poverty-action-report/april-2007/everyone-pays-for-the-uninsured.html>.

CIA World Factbook. 7 Oct. 2007 <https://www.cia.gov/library/publications/the-world-factbook/>

Committee on the Consequences. Hidden Cost Value Lost: The Cost of Uninsurance in America. N.p.: The National Academies Press, 2003. http://www.nap.edu/about.html. 2003. 20 Nov. 2007 <http://www.nap.edu/about.html>.

Dutton, Paul. "France's Model Healthcare System." The Boston Globe 11 Aug. 2007. Boston.Com. 18 Oct. 2007 <http://www.boston.com/news/globe/editorial_opinion/oped/articles/2007/08/11/frances_model_healthcare_system

Green, David, and Benedict Irvine. "Healthcare in France and Germany." Civitas. Dec. 2001. 7 Oct. 2007 <http://civitas.org.uk/pdf/cs17.pdf>.

Health Canada. Health Canada. 18 Oct. 2007 <http://www.hc-sc.gc.ca/hcs-sss/qual/acces/wait-attente/index_e.html>.

Kaiser Family Foundation. Kaiser Family Foundation. 18 Oct. 2007 <http://www.kff.org/insurance/snapshot/chcm010307oth.cfm>.

National Coalition on Health Care. 7 Oct. 2007 <http://nchc.org/facts/coverage.shtml>.

NationMaster. 28 Oct. 2007 <http://www.nationmaster.com/graph/hea_phy_per_1000_peo-physicians-per-1-000-people>.

Physicians for a National Health Program. 6 Oct. 2007 <http://www.pnhp.org/>.

Reiland, Ralph. "Survivors more common in America." Pittsburgh Tribune-Review 28 Feb. 2005. Pittsburgh Tribune-Review. 18 Oct. 2007 <http://www.pittsburghlive.com/x/pittsburghtrib/s_307614.html>.

"The French Lesson In Health Care." Business Week 9 July 2007. Business Week. <http://www.businessweek.com/magazine/content/07_28/b4042070.htm>.

World Health Organization. World Health Organization. 7 Oct. 2007 <http://www.who.int/en/>.

Reflective Overview Assignment

Each Portfolio will include an extensive, well-developed reflective overview

In an extensive, well developed reflective overview—one of the most important pieces of writing in your portfolio—explain to your teachers what you include, why you chose to include what you did, and how those materials represent your learning. This will be more than a mere description of contents. Instead, you will help readers understand how materials you have chosen are evidence of the kinds of learning / participation that you say they are. Include a section in your reflective overview that serves as self-assessment for the portfolio period.

This reflective overview will represent careful, college level writing. It is more than a description. It is also an analysis and an evaluation of the materials. One way to think of the purpose of your overview is to persuade readers that your performance for the period of the portfolio should be evaluated in a certain way, earning a certain grade, with ample reasons to support your claims. Obviously, with this much to accomplish, the overview is important. Effective overviews will be several pages long, well organized, clear.

An "A" reflective letter provides evidence of participation in the full range of class assignments, but particularly focused on the writing processes and decisions you've used or made while writing your project. It is an argument constructed for your composition teacher and your seminar instructor. Specifically for composition, your reflective overview describes and analyzes the writing processes used in the creation of the project document. Overall, the "A" letter serves as detailed proposal for a specific portfolio grade and supports that proposal with ample and appropriate explanation and support. Finally, the letter limits problems with sentencing, punctuation, usage, format, surface mechanics, and other standard conventions so that readers are not distracted by these kinds of problems.

Tim Harlow
December 5, 2007
English

PORTFOLIO THREE REFLECTIVE OVERVIEW

My initial topic choice for portfolio three was coral bleaching, but when I began writing a rough draft I found that the sources on the subject were either scarce of information or very repetitive. With the benefit of hindsight, I now realize I should have been using scientific databases rather than a haphazard Google search, but apparently in my hurry to put together a rough draft, this idea never occurred to me. As a result, I ended up resorting to revising my feature story topic of universal health care to fit the criteria of an argument paper.

Considering my primary self-criticism for the feature story was that it sounded like too much like a watered down research paper, the prospect of presenting previously researched information in an argument format was not exactly a daunting task. I began my first draft by going over the argument paper and deleting all of the "fluff". I took out the entire introduction, the quotes by presidential candidates, and some of the smaller bits of commentary spaced throughout the paper. My additions were a new introduction, small bits of research changes, and a new paragraph about efficiency and administration costs. My critiques for this first draft pointed out some poor sentence structures, incorrect word usages, and suggested that I explain the argument that less profitable health care will lead to less research and poorer technology. I attempted to research this argument for some time with only muddling results. The articles I found in support of this argument tended to simply state that the United States spends more than any other country on medical research, while opposing articles typically attempted to show that much of this research is government funded and wouldn't change regardless of the health care system. The two main questions which I felt would have to be addressed were the actual percentage of health-care technology research that is publically funded in the United States, and how to measure the actual research accomplishments by country. I wrote a paragraph trying to address this problem, but it was of extremely disproportionate length compared to the rest of paper, and didn't come to any real conclusion.

In the second draft I corrected most of the technical errors from the first, added a new paragraph on doctor's opinions about managed care, and wrote a new conclusion. For the final draft I added a paragraph of commentary concerning France's health care system, some new research concerning MRI machines, and yet another conclusion.

The power point show, like the paper, was completed in three drafts. The first of these drafts had no sources or pictures, while the second, which was presented in class, incorporated graphics and slightly cut down on some of the text. The final draft, which was presented at first year celebration contained three more pages, one being a large graph, and the other two mostly text.

Despite being made up mostly of recycled sources, portfolio three required no less effort than the previous two, mostly due to the visual aspect and large amount of peer reviews.